CUTE**NITS**
FOR BABY FEET

The Craft Library

CUTE KNITS
FOR BABY FEET

30 simple projects from
newborn to 4 years

Sue Whiting

hamlyn

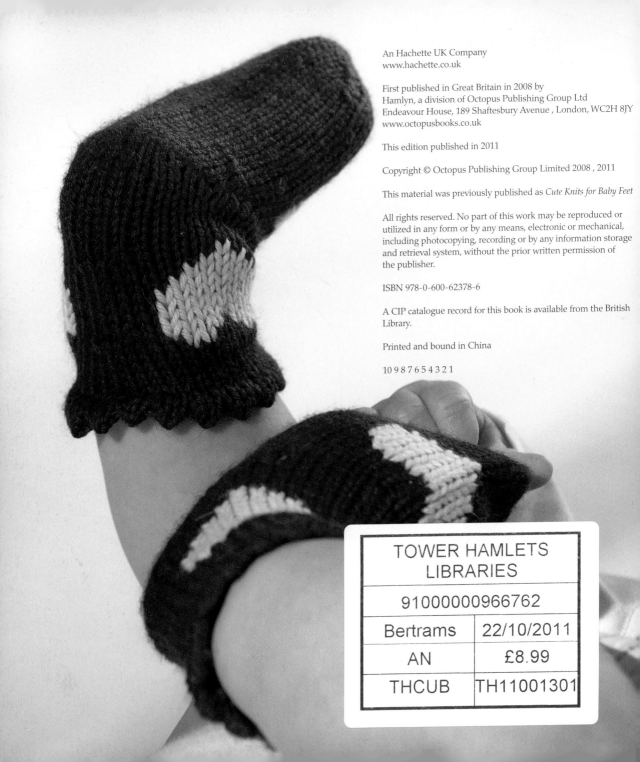

An Hachette UK Company
www.hachette.co.uk

First published in Great Britain in 2008 by
Hamlyn, a division of Octopus Publishing Group Ltd
Endeavour House, 189 Shaftesbury Avenue , London, WC2H 8JY
www.octopusbooks.co.uk

This edition published in 2011

This material was previously published as *Cute Knits for Baby Feet*

ISBN 978-0-600-62378-6

A CIP catalogue record for this book is available from the British
Library.

Printed and bound in China

10 9 8 7 6 5 4 3 2 1

contents

introduction

Making socks for tiny feet is rewarding and fun – and quick and easy, too! Whether you prefer stripes or dots, lace or cable, flowers or balloons, you'll find plenty of favourite styles and new ideas among the 30 designs in this book.

Patterns range from traditional ones, such as Fab Fair Isle on page 100, Classic Rib on page 20 and Sailor Stripes on page 122, to quirky animal designs like Big Ears on page 52 and Snake Socksss on page 66. As all the projects are small, they are a perfect way of trying out new knitting techniques (see page 8), such as intarsia or Swiss darning.

Many of the socks are knitted in the round on four needles, helping you to quickly produce the seven pairs of Socks in a Box on page 104, for example. Tubular knitting means no seams to sew up afterwards – a definite bonus. However, if you prefer to stick to two needles, there are also plenty of designs that are knitted in rows, such as the beautiful Ballet Shoes on page 126, made with luxury yarn and taffeta ribbons.

All the patterns offer a variety of different sizes, so you can keep knitting from the moment your little one is born right up until he or she is four years old. The yarns used have been specially selected for each design, keeping tiny toes cosy in the cold and cool in summer. Most importantly, the socks are soft and comfortable for sensitive feet. And, as almost all these little socks need less than one ball of yarn, they are the perfect way to use up oddments you may have left over from bigger projects.

Every mother knows just how difficult it can be sometimes to get her little one dressed, but with these cute socks the problem may be getting them off, not on. So what's stopping you? Get out your needles and yarn and start knitting now!

techniques

Many of the projects in this book are knitted in the round, using four needles, to create a seam-free sock. Other useful techniques to know are the intarsia method for making vertical colour changes and Swiss darning, in which embroidery stitches are used to add motifs. Grafting is a method of sewing two knitted edges together stitch by stitch, so that the join is invisible.

knitting with four double-pointed needles

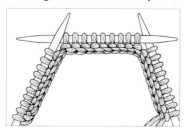 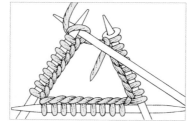 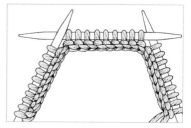

1 Begin by casting on the required number of stitches onto a single-pointed needle of the same size as the double-pointed needles. Slip the stitches onto the double-pointed needles, leaving one needle free for working the stitches. Here, three needles out of a set of four are used.

2 Arrange the needles so that their points cross as shown. Check the stitches are not twisted. Place a ring marker over the point holding the last cast-on stitch. With the remaining needle, knit the first cast-on stitch; draw the yarn firmly to close the gap.

3 Continue working into all the stitches on the first needle. When this needle is free, use it to work into the stitches on the second needle. When the work is the required depth, cast (bind) off as usual. Draw the yarn through the first stitch of the round to make a neat join.

intarsia method

1 When changing colour on a knit row, work in the first colour to the point for the colour change and, if the second colour is being introduced for the first time, tie it to the first colour. On subsequent rows, drop the first colour over the second, pick up the second colour and continue knitting with it. This twists the yarns around each other to avoid leaving a split in the fabric.

2 When changing colour on a purl row, work in the first colour to the point for the colour change. Drop the first colour over the second, pick up the second and continue purling with it.

 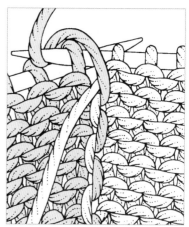

Swiss darning

1 Begin at the bottom-right corner of the motif and fasten the yarn with one or two stitches at the back of the area. Bring the needle up through the base of the first stitch to be embroidered, taking it up to the right, along over the stitch, then under it from right to left, bringing it out as shown in the upper left of the illustration.

2 Take the needle down at the centre of the stitch where it emerged, and then one stitch to the left as show in the lower left of the illustration. Repeat Steps 1 and 2 to cover this and all subsequent stitches. Take care not to pull the stitches tightly.

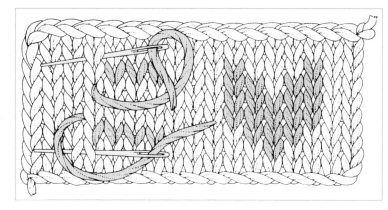

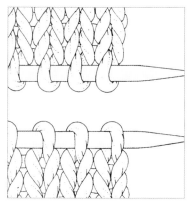

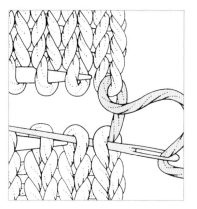

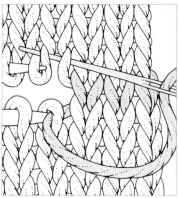

grafting

1 When grafting stocking (stockinette) stitch, end one piece of knitting with a knit row and the other with a purl row, so that when the work is positioned as shown both needles will point to the right.

2 Thread a tapestry needle with matching yarn, three times the length of the knitted edge. Insert the needle purlwise through the first stitch on the lower edge, then purlwise through the opposite stitch on the upper edge. Take it knitwise through the first stitch again, then purlwise through the second stitch on the same edge.

3 *Insert the needle knitwise into the stitch on the upper edge where the yarn emerges, then purlwise into the next stitch to the left. Insert it knitwise into the stitch just below, then purlwise into the next stitch to the left. Repeat from * to end.

warm and woolly

fluffy clouds

Junior will be walking on air in these clever socks featuring fluffy clouds.
They are knitted on two needles using a practical wool and cotton yarn,
and the fluffy clouds are worked in a light-as-air fine mohair.

materials

One 50 g (1¾ oz) ball of Rowan Wool Cotton
in blue (Aloof 958)
One 25 g (⅞ oz) ball of Rowan Kidsilk Haze
in cream (Cream 634)

needles

Pair of 4 mm (UK 8) (US size 6) knitting needles

sizes

to fit age 6–12 [12–18:18–24] mths
length of foot 9.5 [10:10.5] cm (3¾ [4:4¼] in)

tension/gauge

22 sts and 30 rows to 10 cm (4 in) measured over stocking
(stockinette) st using 4 mm (US size 6) needles.

special notes

Use Kidsilk Haze *double* throughout (for clouds).
For Right Sock read odd-numbered (knit) rows of chart
from right to left and even-numbered (purl) rows from
left to right.
For Left Sock read odd-numbered (knit) rows of chart from
left to right and even-numbered (purl) rows from right to
left (to reverse design and make a pair of socks).

abbreviations

K knit; P purl; psso pass slipped stitch over; rem remaining;
rep repeat; RS right side; sl 1 slip one stitch;
st(s) stitch(es); stocking (stockinette) st RS rows K, WS
rows P; tog together; WS wrong side; g grams;
oz ounces; mm millimetres; mths months;
cm centimetres; in inches.

fluffy clouds

Right sock

Using blue, cast on 26 [28:30] sts.

row 1 (RS) Knit.

Rep this row 3 times more.

Starting with a K row, work in stocking (stockinette) st for 2 rows, ending after a WS row.

Using a separate ball of yarn for each block of colour, twisting yarns together on WS where they meet to avoid holes forming and starting and ending rows as indicated, now work following chart as follows:

Work 18 rows, ending after a WS row.

Shape heel

Using blue *only* for heel, work as follows:

row 1 (RS) K12 [13:14], wrap next st (by slipping next st from left needle onto right needle, taking yarn to opposite side of work between needles and then slipping same st back onto left needle; when working back across wrapped sts, work the wrapped st together with any wrapped loops) and turn.

**row 2 Sl 1, P9 [10:11], wrap next st and turn.

row 3 Sl 1, K8 [9:10], wrap next st and turn.

row 4 Sl 1, P7 [8:9], wrap next st and turn.

row 5 Sl 1, K6 [7:8], wrap next st and turn.

row 6 Sl 1, P5 [6:7], wrap next st and turn.

row 7 Rep row 5.

row 8 Rep row 4.

row 9 Rep row 3.

row 10 Rep row 2.

row 11 Sl 1, K10 [11:12], wrap next st and turn.

row 12 Sl 1, P11 [12:13], wrap next st and turn.

row 13 Sl 1, K to end.

Starting with row 20 of chart, work 9 rows, ending after chart row 28.

Complete sock in stocking (stockinette) st using blue only.

Work 8 [10:12] rows, ending after a WS row.

Shape toe

row 1 (RS) K1, (sl 1, K1, psso, K8 [9:10], K2tog) twice, K1. 22 [24:26] sts.

row 2 Purl.

row 3 K1, (sl 1, K1, psso, K6 [7:8], K2tog) twice, K1. 18 [20:22] sts.

row 4 Purl.

row 5 K1, (sl 1, K1, psso, K4 [5:6], K2tog) twice, K1. 14 [16:18] sts.

row 6 Purl.

Cast (bind) off.

Left sock

Work as given for Right Sock to start of heel shaping, remembering to reverse chart as explained in Special Notes.

Shape heel

Using blue *only* for heel, work as follows:

row 1 (RS) K24 [26:28], wrap next st and turn.

Complete as given for Right Sock from **.

Finishing

Press carefully following instructions on yarn label.

Sew inside leg, foot and toe seams.

cast-on edge

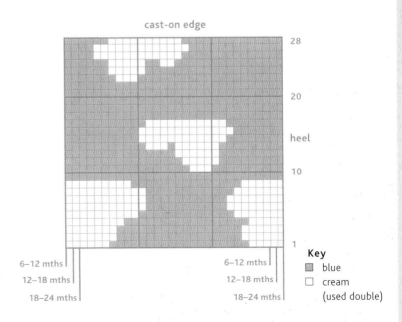

28

20

heel

10

1

6–12 mths

12–18 mths

18–24 mths

6–12 mths

12–18 mths

18–24 mths

Key

▨ blue

☐ cream (used double)

slipper socks

Smart cables cover these cosy slipper socks. Worked on four needles in a soft cashmere blend yarn, they are practical too, because the sole is strengthened with a layer of suede or felt.

materials
One 50 g (1¾ oz) ball of Rowan RYC Cashsoft DK in red (Poppy 512)

extras
Piece of suede or felt measuring 20 cm (7¾ in) by 15 cm (6 in) (for soles) and matching sewing thread. If you have solid floors choose a non-slip fabric for the soles.

tension/gauge
22 sts and 30 rows to 10 cm (4 in) measured over stocking (stockinette) st using 4 mm (US size 6) needles.

needles
Set of 4 double-pointed 4 mm (UK 8) (US size 6) knitting needles
Cable needle

sizes
to fit age 18 mths–2 yrs [2–3 yrs:3–4 yrs]
length of foot 12.5 [13.5:14.5] cm (5 [5¼:5¾] in)

abbreviations
C4B slip next 2 sts onto cable needle and leave at back of work, K2, then K2 from cable needle; inc increase; K knit; P purl; patt pattern or work in pattern; psso pass slipped stitch over; rem remaining; rep repeat; RS right side; sl 1 slip one stitch; st(s) stitch(es); tog together; 0 no stitches worked for this size; g grams; oz ounces; mm millimetres; mths months; yrs years; cm centimetres; in inches.

slipper socks

Socks

(both alike)

Cast on 32 sts.

Distribute these sts over 3 of the needles and, using 4th needle, work in rounds as follows:

round 1 (RS) K1, (P2, K2) 7 times, P2, K1. Rep this round 3 times more.

round 5 Inc once in each of first 3 sts, (P3, inc once in each of next 2 sts) twice, (P2, inc once in each of next 2 sts) twice, (P3, inc once in each of next 2 sts) twice, P1. 47 sts.

round 6 P2, (K4, P3) twice, (K4, P2) twice, (K4, P3) twice, K4, P1.

round 7 P2, (C4B, P3) twice, (C4B, P2) twice, (C4B, P3) twice, C4B, P1.

rounds 8 and 9 Rep round 6.

Rounds 6 to 9 form cable patt.

Work in cable patt for 9 rounds more.

round 19 Patt 13 sts, P2tog, patt 18 sts, P2tog, patt 12 sts. 45 sts.

Size 18 mths–2 yrs only

Keeping patt correct as now set (by working 2 purl sts between cables where decrease was just worked), work 5 rounds.

round 25 Patt 6 sts, P2tog, patt 30 sts, P2tog, patt 5 sts. 43 sts.

Work 4 rounds.

round 30 Patt 6 sts, P2tog, patt 28 sts, P2tog, patt 5 sts. 41 sts.

Keeping patt correct as now set (by working 1 purl st between cables where decrease was just worked), work 4 rounds.

Size 2–3 yrs only

Keeping patt correct as now set (by working 2 purl sts between cables where decrease was just worked), work 7 rounds.

round 27 Patt 6 sts, P2tog, patt 30 sts, P2tog, patt 5 sts. 43 sts.

Work 7 rounds.

Size 3–4 yrs only

Keeping patt correct as now set (by working 2 purl sts between cables where decrease was just worked), work 15 rounds.

All sizes

round 35 P2tog, patt to end. 40 [42:44] sts.

Work 4 [5:6] rounds.

Shape heel

row 1 (RS) K1, (K2tog) twice, K1 [2:3], (K2tog) twice and turn.

Slip next 20 sts of last complete round onto a spare needle and now working in rows, not rounds, work on rem set of sts only for heel as follows:

row 2 P7 [8:9], (P2tog) twice P1 [2:3], (P2tog) twice. 12 [14:16] sts.

row 3 Knit.

row 4 Purl.

rows 5 to 8 (Rep rows 3 and 4) twice.

row 9 K7 [9:11], sl 1, K1, psso and turn.

row 10 P3 [5:7], P2tog and turn.

row 11 K3 [5:7], sl 1, K1, psso and turn.

rows 12 to 15 (Rep rows 10 and 11) twice.

row 16 Rep row 10.

Now starting to work in rounds again, work as follows:

round 16 K4 [6:8], pick up and knit 4 sts down row-end edge of heel, patt 20 sts on spare needle, pick up and knit 4 sts up other row-end edge of heel, K2 [3:4]. Distribute all 32 [34:36] sts over 3 needles and, using 4th needle, now work in rounds

again and shape foot as follows:

next round K6 [7:8], patt 20 sts, K6 [7:8]. Rep last round 23 [25:27] times.

Shape toe

round 1 K8 [9:10], (K2tog) twice, K2, (K2tog) twice, K2, (K2tog) twice, K8 [9:10]. 26 [28:30] sts.

round 2 Knit.

round 3 K4 [5:5], K2tog, sl 1, K1, psso, K10 [10:12], K2tog, sl 1, K1, psso, K4 [5:5]. 22 [24:26] sts.

round 4 Knit.

round 5 K3 [4:4], K2tog, sl 1, K1, psso, K8 [8:10], K2tog, sl 1, K1, psso, K3 [4:4]. 18 [20:22] sts.

round 6 Knit.

round 7 K2 [3:3], K2tog, sl 1, K1, psso, K6 [6:8], K2tog, sl 1, K1, psso, K2 [3:3]. 14 [16:18] sts.

round 8 K3 [16:4], (sl 1, K1, psso, K4 [0:6], K2tog) 1 [0:1] times, K3 [0:4]. 12 [16:16] sts.

round 9 K3 [4:4].

Slip next 6 [8:8] sts onto one needle and rem 6 [8:8] sts onto another needle. Graft the 2 sets of 6 [8:8] sts together to close toe seam.

Finishing

Press carefully following instructions on yarn label.

Cut out two sole shapes (by tracing around sole of sock) from suede or felt, then neatly sew to sole of sock, stitching around entire outer edge.

classic rib

Keep tiny toes snug in these little ribbed socks. Knitted on four needles in a warm and fluffy yarn, the neat turn-back cuff ensures a close fit around the ankle to keep out any chill breezes.

materials

One 50 g (1¾ oz) ball of Rowan RYC Cashcotton 4-Ply in blue (Vivid 908)

needles

Set of 4 double-pointed 3 mm (UK 11) (US size 3) knitting needles

sizes

to fit age 0–3 [3–6:6–12:12–18] mths
length of foot 8.5 [9:9.5:10] cm (3¼ [3½:3¾:4] in)

tension/gauge

28 sts and 36 rows to 10 cm (4 in) measured over stocking (stockinette) st using 3 mm (US size 3) needles.

abbreviations

K knit; P purl; psso pass slipped stitch over; rem remaining; rep repeat; RS right side; sl 1 slip one stitch; st(s) stitch(es); tog together; 0 no stitches or times worked for this size; g grams; oz ounces; mm millimetres; mths months; cm centimetres; in inches.

classic rib

Socks
(both alike)

Cast on 30 [32:34:36] sts.

Distribute these sts over 3 of the needles and, using 4th needle, work in rounds as follows:

round 1 (RS) P0 [1:2:1], *K2, P2, rep from * to last 2 [3:0:3] sts, K2 [2:0:2], P0 [1:0:1]. This round forms rib.

Work in rib for 27 [29:31:33] rounds more.

Shape heel

row 1 (RS) K5 [6:7:6], wrap next st (by slipping next st from left needle onto right needle, taking yarn to opposite side of work between needles and then slipping same st back onto left needle – when working back across wrapped sts, work the wrapped st together with any wrapped loops) and turn.

Slip next 18 [18:18:22] sts of last complete round onto a spare needle and now working in rows, not rounds, work on rem set of 12 [14:16:14] sts only for heel as follows:

row 2 Sl 1, P9 [11:13:11], wrap next st and turn.

row 3 Sl 1, K8 [10:12:10], wrap next st and turn.

row 4 Sl 1, P7 [9:11:9], wrap next st and turn.

row 5 Sl 1, K6 [8:10:8], wrap next st and turn.

row 6 Sl 1, P5 [7:9:7], wrap next st and turn.

row 7 Sl 1, K4 [6:8:6], wrap next st and turn.

row 8 Sl 1, P3 [5:7:5], wrap next st and turn.

row 9 Rep row 7.

row 10 Rep row 6.

row 11 Rep row 5.

row 12 Rep row 4.

row 13 Rep row 3.

row 14 Rep row 2.

row 15 Sl 1, K10 [12:14:12], wrap next st and turn.

row 16 Sl 1, P11 [13:15:13], wrap next st (first stitch from spare needle) and turn.

row 17 Sl 1, K5 [6:7:6].

Distribute all 30 [32:34:36] sts over 3 needles and, using 4th needle, now work in rounds again and shape foot as follows:

next round (RS) K6 [7:8:7], (P2, K2) 4 [4:4:5] times, P2, K6 [7:8:7].

Rep last round 17 [19:21:23] times more.

Shape toe

round 1 (K7 [0:8:0], sl 1, K1, psso, K12 [0:14:0], K2tog) 1 [0:1:0] times, K7 [32:8:36]. 28 [32:32:36] sts.

round 2 Knit.

round 3 K5 [6:6:7], K2tog, sl 1, K1, psso, K10 [12:12:14], K2tog, sl 1, K1, psso, K5 [6:6:7]. 24 [28:28:32] sts.

round 4 Knit.

round 5 K4 [5:5:6], K2tog, sl 1, K1, psso, K8 [10:10:12], K2tog, sl 1, K1, psso, K4 [5:5:6]. 20 [24:24:28] sts.

round 6 Knit.

round 7 K3 [4:4:5], K2tog, sl 1, K1, psso, K6 [8:8:10], K2tog, sl 1, K1, psso, K3 [4:4:5]. 16 [20:20:24] sts.

round 8 Knit.

round 9 K4 [5:5:6].

Slip next 8 [10:10:12] sts onto one needle and rem 8 [10:10:12] sts onto another needle. Graft the 2 sets of 8 [10:10:12] sts together to close toe seam.

Finishing

Press carefully following instructions on yarn label.

Fold cuff to outside around upper edge.

christmas stocking

Adorned with reindeer, trees and snowflakes, this perfect Christmas stocking is sure to bring joy to any little angel on Christmas morning. Knitted in two identical pieces, it is lined to keep presents well hidden inside.

materials

One 50 g (1¾ oz) ball of Rowan Kid Classic in each of black (Smoke 831), red (Cherry Red 847), green (Spruce 853) and cream (Feather 828)

extras

Piece of lining fabric 50 cm (20 in) by 40 cm (16 in) and matching sewing thread

needles

Pair of 4.5 mm (UK 7) (US size 7) knitting needles

sizes

Completed stocking is 22 cm (8¾ in) at widest point and 33 cm (13 in) long.

tension/gauge

19 sts and 25 rows to 10 cm (4 in) measured over stocking (stockinette) st using 4.5 mm (US size 7) needles.

special note

When working in pattern, strand yarn not in use across WS of work. For First Side, read odd-numbered (knit) rows right to left; even-numbered (purl) rows left to right. For Second Side, read odd-numbered (knit) rows left to right; even-numbered (purl) rows right to left (to reverse design).

abbreviations

alt alternate; beg beginning; dec decrease; foll following; inc increase; K knit; P purl; rem remaining; rep repeat; RS right side; st(s) stitch(es); stocking (stockinette) st RS rows K, WS rows P; WS wrong side; g grams; oz ounces; mm millimetres; cm centimetres; in inches.

christmas stocking

First side

Using black, cast on 18 sts.

Starting with a K row, now work in stocking (stockinette) st following chart as follows:

Work 1 row.

Inc 1 st at end of next row and at same (heel) edge on foll 13 rows, then on foll 2 alt rows *and at same time* inc 1 st at beg of next row and at same (toe) edge of foll 3 rows, then on foll 3 alt rows, ending after a RS row. 41 sts.

Work 1 row.

Dec 1 st at toe edge of next and foll alt row, then on foll 8 rows, then on foll 2 alt rows, then on foll 4th row *and at same time* inc

1 st at heel edge of next row. 29 sts.

Work 37 rows, ending after chart row 76.

Using black, knit 2 rows.

Using red, knit 2 rows.

Using green, knit 2 rows.

Using black, knit 1 row.

Cast (bind) off knitwise (on WS).

Second side

Work as given for First Side reversing shaping and chart.

Hanging loop

Using red, cast on 22 sts.

Using red, knit 2 rows.

Using cream, knit 2 rows.

Using red, knit 1 row.

Cast (bind) off knitwise (on WS).

Finishing

Press carefully following instructions on yarn label.

From lining fabric, cut out two pieces the same size as knitted Sides, adding seam allowance along all edges.

Sew together knitted pieces along cast-on and row-end edges, leaving cast-off (bound-off) edges open. Fold Hanging Loop in half and attach to inside of upper edge against back seam.

Sew together lining pieces in same way as knitted pieces and slip lining inside stocking. Turn under raw edge around upper opening edge and slip stitch in place.

cast-on edge

Key
- ■ black
- ■ red
- ■ green
- □ cream

woolly tights

These roomy woolly tights are designed for baby's comfort.
Knitted in a tweedy yarn on four needles, they have no seams, and the
neat elastic casing at the waist will keep them firmly in place.

materials

Two 50 g (1¾ oz) balls of Rowan Felted Tweed
in pink (Clover 162)

extras

Waist length of 15 mm (⅝ in) wide elastic

needles

Set of 4 double-pointed 4 mm (UK 8) (US size 6)
knitting needles

sizes

to fit age 0–3 [3–6:6–12:12–18] mths
length of foot 8.5 [9:9.5:10] cm (3¼ [3½:3¾:4] in)

tension/gauge

22 sts and 30 rows to 10 cm (4 in) measured over stocking
(stockinette) st using 4 mm (US size 6) needles.

abbreviations

alt alternate; dec decrease; foll following; inc increase;
K knit; M1 make one stitch by picking up loop lying
between needles and working into back of this loop;
P purl; psso pass slipped stitch over; rem remaining;
rep repeat; RS right side; sl 1 slip one stitch; st(s) stitch(es);
stocking (stockinette) st RS rows K, WS rows P; tog together; WS wrong side; g grams; oz ounces;
mm millimetres; mths months; cm centimetres; in inches.

woolly tights

Tights

Cast on 96 [104:112:120] sts.

Distribute these sts over 3 of the needles and, using 4th needle, work in rounds as follows:

round 1 (RS) *K1, P1, rep from * to end. Rep this round 5 times more.

Shape back

row 1 (RS) K37 [40:43:46], wrap next st (by slipping next st from left needle onto right needle, taking yarn to opposite side of work between needles and then slipping same st back onto left needle – when working back across wrapped sts, work the wrapped st together with any wrapped loops) and turn.

row 2 Sl 1, P73 [79:85:91], wrap next st and turn.

row 3 Sl 1, K66 [71:76:81], wrap next st and turn.

row 4 Sl 1, P59 [63:67:71], wrap next st and turn.

row 5 Sl 1, K52 [55:58:61], wrap next st and turn.

row 6 Sl 1, P45 [47:49:51], wrap next st and turn.

row 7 Sl 1, K38 [39:40:41], wrap next st and turn.

row 8 Sl 1, P31, wrap next st and turn.

row 9 Sl 1, K15.

This completes back shaping.

Now working in rounds, not rows, work as follows:

next round Knit.

This round forms stocking (stockinette) st. Work in stocking (stockinette) st for 39 [41:43:45] rounds more.

Shape crotch

Place marker on needle after 48th [52nd:56th:60th] st – this is centre front.

next round K1, M1, K to within 1 st of marker, M1, K2 (marker is between these 2 sts), M1, K to last st, M1, K1. 100 [108:116:124] sts.

Working all increases as set by last round, work as follows:

Work 3 rounds.

Inc 4 sts (1 st at beginning, 1 st at end, and 1 st either side of centre front marker) on next round, then on foll 2 alt rounds, then on foll 3 rounds. 124 [132:140:148] sts.

Divide for legs

next round K to marker.

Slip rem 62 [66:70:74] sts onto a holder for left leg and work on this first set of 62 [66:70:74] sts only for right leg.

Distribute these 62 [66:70:74] sts over 3 needles and, using 4th needle, now work in rounds as follows:

next round Sl 1, K1, psso, K to last 2 sts, K2tog. 60 [64:68:72] sts.

Working all decreases as set by last round, dec 1 st at each end of next 7 rounds, then on foll 7 alt rounds, then on 2 [3:4:5] foll 4th rounds, then on 2 foll 6th rounds. 24 [26:28:30] sts.

Work 11 [13:15:17] rounds. (Adjust leg length here if required.)

woolly tights

Shape heel

row 1 (RS) Sl 1, K10 [11:12:13], wrap next st and turn.

Slip next 12 [13:14:15] sts of last complete round onto a spare needle and now working in rows, not rounds, work on rem set of 12 [13:14:15] sts only for heel as follows:

row 2 Sl 1, P9 [10:11:12], wrap next st and turn.

row 3 Sl 1, K8 [9:10:11], wrap next st and turn.

row 4 Sl 1, P7 [8:9:10], wrap next st and turn.

row 5 Sl 1, K6 [7:8:9], wrap next st and turn.

row 6 Sl 1, P5 [6:7:8], wrap next st and turn.

row 7 Rep row 5.

row 8 Rep row 4.

row 9 Rep row 3.

row 10 Rep row 2.

row 11 Rep row 1.

row 12 Sl 1, P11 [12:13:14], wrap next st (first stitch from spare needle) and turn.

Distribute all 24 [26:28:30] sts over 3 needles and, using 4th needle, now work in rounds again and shape foot as follows: Work 14 [16:18:20] rounds.

Shape toe

round 1 (Sl 1, K1, psso, K8 [9:10:11], K2tog) twice. 20 [22:24:26] sts.

round 2 Knit.

round 3 (Sl 1, K1, psso, K6 [7:8:9], K2tog) twice. 16 [18:20:22] sts.

round 4 Knit.

round 5 (Sl 1, K1, psso, K4 [5:6:7], K2tog) twice. 12 [14:16:18] sts.

round 6 Knit.

Slip first 6 [7:8:9] sts onto one needle and last 6 [7:8:9] sts onto another needle. Graft the 2 sets of 6 [7:8:9] sts together to close toe seam.

Shape left leg

Return to sts left on holder and distribute these 62 [66:70:74] sts over 3 needles and, using 4th needle, now work in rounds as follows:

next round Sl 1, K1, psso, K to last 2 sts, K2tog. 60 [64:68:72] sts.

Working all decreases as set by last round, dec 1 st at each end of next 7 rounds, then on foll 7 alt rounds, then on 2 [3:4:5] foll 4th rounds, then on 2 foll 6th rounds. 24 [26:28:30] sts.

Work 11 [13:15:17] rounds. (Adjust leg length here if required.)

Shape heel

row 1 (RS) K23 [25:27:29], wrap next st and turn.

Slip first 12 [13:14:15] sts of last complete round onto a spare needle and now working in rows, not rounds, work on rem set of 12 [13:14:15] sts only for heel as follows:

row 2 Sl 1, P9 [10:11:12], wrap next st and turn.

row 3 Sl 1, K8 [9:10:11], wrap next st and turn.

row 4 Sl 1, P7 [8:9:10], wrap next st and turn.

row 5 Sl 1, K6 [7:8:9], wrap next st and turn.

row 6 Sl 1, P5 [6:7:8], wrap next st and turn.

row 7 Rep row 5.

row 8 Rep row 4.

row 9 Rep row 3.

row 10 Rep row 2.

row 11 Sl 1, K10 [11:12:13], wrap next st and turn.

row 12 Sl 1, P11 [12:13:14], wrap next st (first stitch from spare needle) and turn.

Distribute all 24 [26:28:30] sts over 3 needles and, using 4th needle, now work in rounds again and shape foot as follows: Work 14 [16:18:20] rounds.

Complete as given for right leg from start of toe shaping.

Finishing

Press carefully following instructions on yarn label.

Sew together ends of elastic securely. Make a herringbone stitch casing on inside of waist ribbing enclosing elastic.

rainy day

Keep tiny toes comfortable inside their boots with these jaunty socks.
The leg section is knitted on two needles and features the umbrella motif.
At the ankle you change to four needles and knit the rest in rounds.

materials
Two 50 g (1¾ oz) balls of Rowan RYC Cashsoft Aran
in blue (Tornado 008)
Small amount of same yarn in each of red (Poppy 010)
and black (Black 011) for umbrellas

needles
Pair of 4.5 mm (UK 7) (US size 7) knitting needles
Set of 4 double-pointed 4.5 mm (UK 7) (US size 7)
knitting needles

sizes
to fit age 18 mths–2 yrs [2–3 yrs:3–4 yrs]
length of foot 12.5 [13.5:14.5] cm (5 [5¼:5 3/4] in)

tension/gauge
19 sts and 25 rows to 10 cm (4 in) measured over stocking
(stockinette) st using 4.5 mm (US size 7) needles.

abbreviations
inc increase; K knit; P purl; psso pass slipped stitch over;
rem remaining; rep repeat; RS right side;
sl 1 slip one stitch; st(s) stitch(es);
stocking (stockinette) st RS rows K, WS rows P;
tbl through back of loops; tog together; WS wrong side;
g grams; oz ounces; mm millimetres; mths months;
yrs years; cm centimetres; in inches.

rainy day

Right sock

Using pair of needles and blue, cast on 30 [32:34] sts.

row 1 (RS) *K1, P1, rep from * to end.

Rep last row once more.

row 3 K1, inc in next st, K to last 3 sts, inc in next st, K2. 32 [34:36] sts.

Starting with a *purl* row, work in stocking (stockinette) st for 1 row, ending after a WS row.**

Using a separate ball of yarn for each block of colour and twisting yarns together on WS where they meet to avoid holes forming, now place motif chart as follows:

row 5 (RS) K5 [6:7], work next 22 sts following row 1 of chart and reading chart from right to left, K to end.

row 6 P5 [6:7], work next 22 sts following row 2 of chart reading chart from left to right, P to end.

These 2 rows set position of chart.

***Keeping chart correct, cont as follows:

Work 12 rows.

row 19 (RS) K2, sl 1, K1, psso, patt to last 4 sts, K2tog, K2. 30 [32:34] sts.

Work 5 rows.

Rep last 6 rows once more, then row 19 again. 26 [28:30] sts.

Work 1 row. (All 28 rows of chart now completed.)

Working in stocking (stockinette) st using blue only, complete sock as follows:

Work 7 rows, ending after a *RS* row.

row 40 (WS) P2tog tbl, P to last 2 sts, P2tog. 24 [26:28] sts.

Shape heel

Slip first 6 [6:7] sts of next row onto one double-pointed needle and last 6 [7:7] sts onto another double-pointed needle, then slip rem centre 12 [13:14] sts onto a spare needle.

Working in rows, not rounds, work on the 2 sets of sts on double-pointed needles (12 [13:14] sts in total) only for heel as follows:

row 1 (RS) K5 [5:6], wrap next st (by slipping next st from left needle onto right needle, taking yarn to opposite side of work between needles and then slipping same st back onto left needle – when working back across wrapped sts, work the wrapped st together with any wrapped loops) and turn.

row 2 Sl 1, P9 [10:11], wrap next st and turn.

row 3 Sl 1, K8 [9:10], wrap next st and turn.

row 4 Sl 1, P7 [8:9], wrap next st and turn.

row 5 Sl 1, K6 [7:8], wrap next st and turn.

row 6 Sl 1, P5 [6:7], wrap next st and turn.

row 7 Sl 1, K4 [5:6], wrap next st and turn.

row 8 Sl 1, P3 [4:5], wrap next st and turn.

row 9 Rep row 7.

row 10 Rep row 6.

row 11 Rep row 5.

row 12 Rep row 4.

row 13 Rep row 3.

row 14 Rep row 2.

row 15 Sl 1, K10 [11:12], wrap next st (first st from spare needle) and turn.

row 16 Sl 1, P11 [12:13], wrap next st and turn.

row 17 Sl 1, K5 [6:6].

Distribute all 24 [26:28] sts over 3 needles and, using 4th needle, now work in rounds and shape foot as follows:

next round (RS) Knit.

This round forms stocking (stockinette) st (K every round).

Work 19 [21:23] rounds.

Shape toe

round 1 K4 [4:5], K2tog, sl 1, K1, psso, K8 [9:10], K2tog, sl 1, K1, psso, K4 [5:5]. 20 [22:24] sts.

round 2 Knit.

round 3 K3 [3:4], K2tog, sl 1, K1, psso, K6 [7:8], K2tog, sl 1, K1, psso, K3 [4:4]. 16 [18:20] sts.

round 4 Knit.

round 5 K2 [2:3], K2tog, sl 1, K1, psso, K4 [5:6], K2tog, sl 1, K1, psso, K2 [3:3]. 12 [14:16] sts.

round 6 K1 [1:2], K2tog, sl 1, K1, psso, K2 [3:4], K2tog, sl 1, K1, psso, K1 [2:2]. 8 [10:12] sts.

round 7 K2 [3:3].

Slip next 4 [5:6] sts onto one needle and rem 4 [5:6] sts onto another needle. Graft

the 2 sets of 4 [5:6] sts together to close toe seam.

Left sock

Work as given for First Sock to **.

Using a separate ball of yarn for each block of colour and twisting yarns together on WS where they meet to avoid holes forming, now place motif chart as follows:

row 5 (RS) K5 [6:7], work next 22 sts following row 1 of chart reading chart from left to right (to reverse motif), K to end.

row 6 P5 [6:7], work next 22 sts following row 2 of chart and reading chart from right to left, P to end.

These 2 rows set position of chart.

Complete as given for Right Sock from ***.

Finishing

Sew back leg seam. Using black, and photograph as a guide, embroider spines onto umbrellas in stem stitch.

Press carefully following instructions on yarn label.

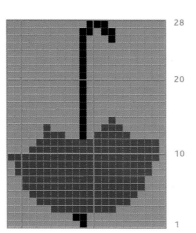

cast-on edge

Key

▓	blue
▨	red
■	black

bobble socks

Tiny contrasting bobbles adorn these cute ankle socks and add a little texture.
To give the pair that one-off look, use a separate length of yarn
for each bobble and make them in lots of different colours.

materials

One 50 g (1¾ oz) ball of Rowan RYC Cashsoft 4-Ply
in each of pale green (Spring 428)
and cream (Cream 433)

needles

Set of 4 double-pointed 3.25 mm (UK 10) (US size 3)
knitting needles

sizes

to fit age 0–3 [3–6:6–12:12–18] mths
length of foot 8.5 [9:9.5:10] cm (3¼ [3½:3¾:4] in)

tension/gauge

28 sts and 36 rows to 10 cm (4 in) measured over stocking
(stockinette) st using 3.25 mm (US size 3) needles.

abbreviations

K knit; MB make bobble using cream as follows – (K1, yfwd,
K1) all into next st, turn, P3, turn, K3, turn, P3, turn, sl 1,
K2tog, psso; P purl; psso pass slipped stitch over; rem
remaining; rep repeat; RS right side; sl 1 slip one stitch;
st(s) stitch(es); tog together; stocking (stockinette) st RS
rows K, WS rows P; WS wrong side; yfwd yarn forward –
bring yarn forward between needles and over right needle
to make a new stitch (US yarn over); 0 no stitches worked
for this size; g grams; oz ounces; mm millimetres; mths
months; cm centimetres; in inches.

bobble socks

Socks

(both alike)

Using pale green, cast on 30 [32:34:36] sts. Distribute these sts over 3 of the needles and, using 4th needle, work in rounds as follows:

round 1 (RS) *K1, P1, rep from * to end. Rep this round 4 times more.

round 6 Knit.

This round forms stocking (stockinette) st. Work in stocking (stockinette) st for 1 [1:2:2] more rounds.

Join in cream and now work in bobble patt as follows:

round 1 K2 [3:4:5], MB, (K5, MB) 4 [4:4:5] times, K3 [4:5:0].

(*Note:* Cream is used for bobbles only – work all other sts using pale green. Strand cream loosely across WS of work from one bobble to next, weaving it in every 2 or 3 sts.)

rounds 2 to 6 Knit.

round 7 K5 [6:1:2], (MB, K5) 4 [4:5:5] times, K0 [1:0:0], MB, K0 [0:2:3].

rounds 8 to 12 Knit.

round 13 Rep round 1.

rounds 14 and 15 Knit.

Shape heel

row 1 (RS) K7 [8:8:9], wrap next st (by slipping next st from left needle onto right needle, taking yarn to opposite side of work between needles and then slipping same st back onto left needle – when working back across wrapped sts, work the wrapped st together with any wrapped loops) and turn. Slip next 15 [16:17:18] sts of last complete round onto a spare needle and now work-ing in rows, not rounds, work on rem set of 15 [16:17:18] sts only for heel as follows:

row 2 Sl 1, P12 [13:14:15], wrap next st and turn.

row 3 Sl 1, K11 [12:13:14], wrap next st and turn.

row 4 Sl 1, P10 [11:12:13], wrap next st and turn.

row 5 Sl 1, K9 [10:11:12], wrap next st and turn.

row 6 Sl 1, P8 [9:10:11], wrap next st and turn.

row 7 Sl 1, K7 [8:9:10], wrap next st and turn.

row 8 Sl 1, P6 [7:8:9], wrap next st and turn.

row 9 Rep row 7.

row 10 Rep row 6.

row 11 Rep row 5.

row 12 Rep row 4.

row 13 Rep row 3.

row 14 Rep row 2.

row 15 Sl 1, K13 [14:15:16], wrap next st and turn.

row 16 Sl 1, P14 [15:16:17], wrap next st (first stitch on spare needle) and turn.

row 17 Sl 1, K6 [6:7:7].

Distribute all 30 [32:34:36] sts over 3 needles and, using 4th needle, now work in rounds again and shape foot as follows:

rounds 1 to 3 Knit.

round 4 K11 [12:13:14], MB, K5, MB, K12 [13:14:15].

rounds 5 to 9 Knit.

round 10 K8 [9:10:11], MB, (K5, MB) twice, K9 [10:11:12].

rounds 11 to 15 Knit.

round 16 Rep round 4.

Break off cream.

Work in stocking (stockinette) st for 6 [8:10:12] rounds.

Shape toe

round 1 K6 [7:7:8], K2tog, sl 1, K1, psso, K11 [12:13:14], K2tog, sl 1, K1, psso, K5 [5:6:6]. 26 [28:30:32] sts.

round 2 Knit.

round 3 K5 [6:6:7], K2tog, sl 1, K1, psso, K9 [10:11:12], K2tog, sl 1, K1, psso, K4 [4:5:5]. 22 [24:26:28] sts.

round 4 Knit.

round 5 K4 [5:5:6], K2tog, sl 1, K1, psso, K7 [8:9:10], K2tog, sl 1, K1, psso, K3 [3:4:4]. 18 [20:22:24] sts.

round 6 K3 [4:4:5], K2tog, sl 1, K1, psso, K5 [6:7:8], K2tog, sl 1, K1, psso, K2 [2:3:3]. 14 [16:18:20] sts.

round 7 K4 [5:5:6].

Slip next 7 [8:9:10] sts onto one needle and rem 7 [8:9:10] sts onto another needle. Graft the 2 sets of 7 [8:9:10] sts together to close toe seam.

Finishing

Press carefully following instructions on yarn label.

bright stripes

Here's a pair guaranteed to keep tiny toes really warm! Loosely knitted on four needles using a pure wool yarn, they are washed once completed to felt the knitting and shrink them to the right size.

materials

One 25 g (⅞ oz) ball of Rowan Scottish Tweed 4-Ply in each of purple (Lavender 005), orange (Sunset 011), green (Apple 015) and grey (Storm Grey 004)

needles

Set of 4 double-pointed 4 mm (UK 8) (US size 6) knitting needles

sizes

to fit age 6–12 [12–18:18–24] mths
length of foot 9.5 [10:10.5] cm (3¾ [4:4¼] in)

tension/gauge

before washing/shrinking: 18 ½ sts and 27 rows to 10 cm (4 in) measured over stocking (stockinette) st using 4mm (US size 6) needles.
after washing/shrinking: 24 ½ sts and 39 rows to 10 cm (4 in) measured over stocking (stockinette) st using 4 mm (US size 6) needles.

special note

When first knitted, socks will appear far too large and saggy but, once washed, they will shrink to the correct size.

abbreviations

inc increase; K knit; P purl; psso pass slipped stitch over; rem remaining; rep repeat; RS right side; sl 1 slip one stitch; st(s) stitch(es); tog together; WS wrong side; 0 no stitches worked for this size; g grams; oz ounces; mm millimetres; mths months; cm centimetres; in inches.

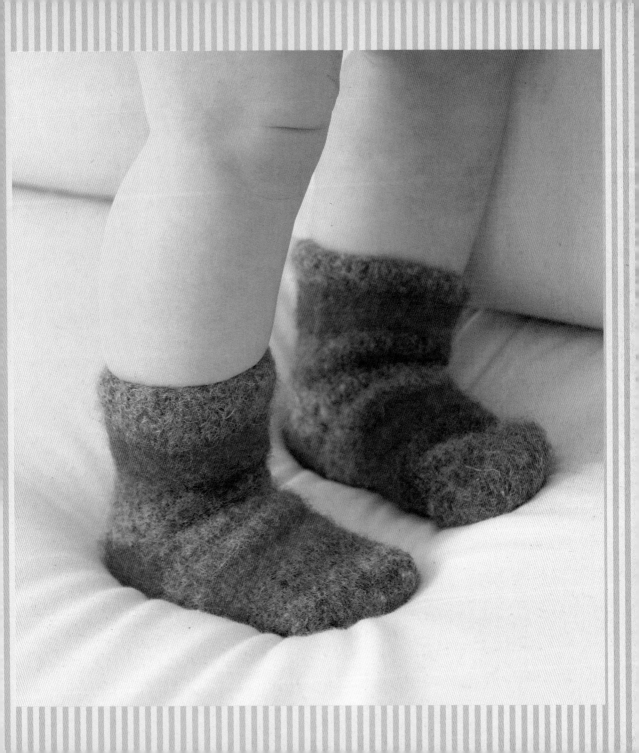

bright stripes

Socks

(both alike)

Using purple, cast on 32 [34:36] sts.
Distribute these sts over 3 of the needles
and, using 4th needle, work in rounds
as follows:

round 1 (RS) *K1, P1, rep from * to end.
Rep this round 3 times more.

round 5 Inc in first st, K to last 2 sts, inc in
next st, K1. 34 [36:38] sts.

rounds 6 to 8 Using purple, knit.
Breaking off old colour and joining in new
colour, now work in stripes as follows:

rounds 9 to 16 Using orange, knit.

rounds 17 and 18 Using green, knit.

round 19 Using green, sl 1, K1, psso, K to
last 3 [2:3] sts, K2tog, K1 [0:1]. 32 [34:36]
sts.

rounds 20 to 24 Using green, knit.

rounds 25 and 26 Using grey, knit.

round 27 Using grey, sl 1, K1, psso, K to
last 3 [2:3] sts, K2tog, K1 [0:1]. 30 [32:34]
sts.

rounds 28 to 32 Using grey, knit.

Shape heel

Slip first 7 [8:8] sts and last 8 [8:9] sts onto
one needle (for heel) and leave rem 15
[16:17] sts on a spare needle.

Now working in rows, not rounds, work on
heel set of 15 [16:17] sts only using orange
as follows:

row 1 (RS) K14 [15:16], wrap next st (by
slipping next st from left needle onto right
needle, taking yarn to opposite side of
work between needles and then slipping
same st back onto left needle – when
working back across wrapped sts, work the
wrapped st together with any wrapped

loops) and turn.

row 2 Sl 1, P12 [13:14], wrap next st
and turn.

row 3 Sl 1, K11 [12:13], wrap next st
and turn.

row 4 Sl 1, P10 [11:12], wrap next st
and turn.

row 5 Sl 1, K9 [10:11], wrap next st
and turn.

row 6 Sl 1, P8 [9:10], wrap next st
and turn.

row 7 Sl 1, K7 [8:9], wrap next st and turn.

row 8 Sl 1, P6 [7:8], wrap next st and turn.

row 9 Rep row 7.

row 10 Rep row 6.

row 11 Rep row 5.

row 12 Rep row 4.

row 13 Rep row 3.

row 14 Rep row 2.

row 15 Sl 1, K13 [14:15], wrap next st
and turn.

row 16 Sl 1, P14 [15:16] and turn.

Slip last 7 [8:8] sts of last row onto one
needle – this marks start and end point of
rounds for foot.

Making sure rounds start and end as now
positioned, distribute all 30 [32:34] sts over
3 needles and, using 4th needle, now work
in rounds again and shape foot as follows:
Using purple, knit 8 rounds.
Using orange, knit 8 rounds.
Using green, knit 8 rounds.
Using grey, knit 8 rounds.

Shape toe

Break off grey and complete sock using
purple *only*.
Work 0 [2:4] rounds.

next round K5 [6:6], K2tog, sl 1, K1, psso,

K11 [12:13], K2tog, sl 1, K1, psso, K6 [6:7].
26 [28:30] sts.

next round Knit.

next round K4 [5:5], K2tog, sl 1, K1, psso,
K9 [10:11], K2tog, sl 1, K1, psso, K5 [5:6].
22 [24:26] sts.

next round Knit.

next round K3 [4:4], K2tog, sl 1, K1, psso,
K7 [8:9], K2tog, sl 1, K1, psso, K4 [4:5]. 18
[20:22] sts.

next round Knit.

next round K4 [5:5].

Slip next 9 [10:11] sts onto one needle and
rem 9 [10:11] sts onto another needle.
Graft the 2 sets of 9 [10:11] sts together to
close toe seam.

Finishing

Do *not* press.

Machine wash socks at 40°C (105°F) to
shrink socks to correct size. Once washed,
ease into correct size and shape and leave
to dry naturally laid flat. (If first wash does
not shrink socks the required amount,
repeat the process carefully until required
size is achieved.)

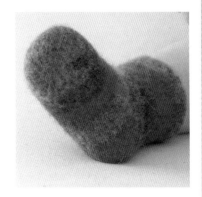

animal magic

gone fishing

There's no need to go fishing to get junior a goldfish. Simply knit these cute cotton socks in one colour using four needles, and then embroider on the sweet little goldfish blowing bubbles.

materials

One 50g (1¾ oz) ball of Rowan 4-Ply Cotton in blue (Bluebell 136)

Small amounts of same yarn in orange (Mandarine 142) and white (Bleached 113) for embroidery

needles

Set of 4 double-pointed 3.25 mm (UK 10) (US size 3) knitting needles

sizes

to fit age 6–12 [12–18:18–24] mths

length of foot 9.5 [10:10.5] cm (3¾ [4:4¼] in)

tension/gauge

28 sts and 38 rows to 10 cm (4 in) measured over stocking (stockinette) st using 3.25 mm (US size 3) needles.

abbreviations

K knit; P purl; psso pass slipped stitch over; rem remaining; rep repeat; RS right side; sl 1 slip one stitch; st(s) stitch(es); tbl through back of loop; stocking (stockinette) st RS rows K, WS rows P; tog together; WS wrong side; g grams; oz ounces; mm millimetres; mths months; cm centimetres; in inches.

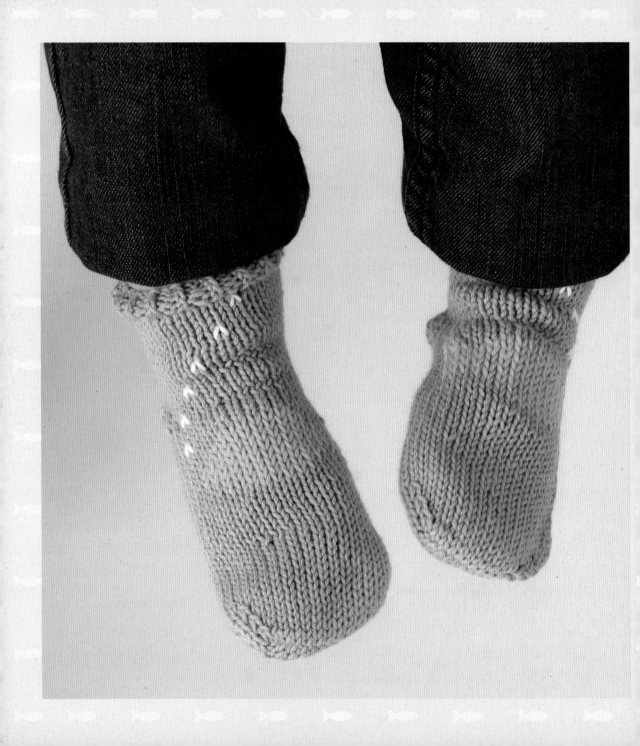

Socks

(both alike)

Using blue, cast on 34 [36:38] sts.
Distribute these sts over 3 of the needles
and, using 4th needle, work in rounds as
follows:

round 1 (RS) *K1 tbl, P1, rep from * to
end.

Rep this round 3 times more.

round 5 Knit.

This round forms stocking (stockinette) st.
Work in stocking (stockinette) st for 17
more rounds.

Shape heel

row 1 (RS) K7 [8:8], wrap next st (by
slipping next st from left needle onto right
needle, taking yarn to opposite side of work
between needles and then slipping same st
back onto left needle – when working back
across wrapped sts, work the wrapped st
together with any wrapped loops) and turn.
Slip next 17 [18:19] sts of last complete
round onto a spare needle and now
working in rows, not rounds, work on rem
set of 17 [18:19] sts only for heel as follows:

row 2 Sl 1, P14 [15:16], wrap next st
and turn.

row 3 Sl 1, K13 [14:15], wrap next st
and turn.

row 4 Sl 1, P12 [13:14], wrap next st
and turn.

row 5 Sl 1, K11 [12:13], wrap next st
and turn.

row 6 Sl 1, P10 [11:12], wrap next st
and turn.

row 7 Sl 1, K9 [10:11], wrap next st and
turn.

row 8 Sl 1, P8 [9:10], wrap next st and turn.

row 9 Rep row 7.

row 10 Rep row 6.

row 11 Rep row 5.

row 12 Rep row 4.

row 13 Rep row 3.

row 14 Rep row 2.

row 15 Sl 1, K15 [16:17], wrap next st
and turn.

row 16 Sl 1, P16 [17:18], wrap next st
(first stitch on spare needle) and turn.

row 17 Sl 1, K8 [8:9].

Distribute all 34 [36:38] sts over 3 needles
and, using 4th needle, now work in rounds
again and shape foot as follows:
Work in stocking (stockinette) st for 28
[30:32] rounds.

Shape toe

round 1 K6 [7:7], K2tog, sl 1, K1, psso, K13
[14:15], K2tog, sl 1, K1, psso, K7 [7:8]. 30
[32:34] sts.

round 2 Knit.

round 3 K5 [6:6], K2tog, sl 1, K1, psso, K11
[12:13], K2tog, sl 1, K1, psso, K6 [6:7]. 26
[28:30] sts.

round 4 Knit.

round 5 K4 [5:5], K2tog, sl 1, K1, psso, K9
[10:11], K2tog, sl 1, K1, psso, K5 [5:6]. 22
[24:26] sts.

round 6 Knit.

round 7 K5 [6:6].

Slip next 11 [12:13] sts onto one needle
and rem 11 [12:13] sts onto another
needle. Graft the 2 sets of 11 [12:13] sts
together to close toe seam.

Finishing

Following chart, Swiss darn (duplicate
stitch) motif onto socks – place chart

centrally on top of foot starting 7 rounds
down from cast-on edge and reverse chart
for second sock to make a pair.
Press following instructions on yarn label.

cast-on edge

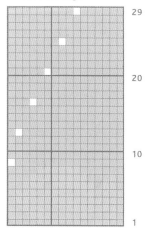

Key

☐ blue
☐ orange (Swiss darning)
☐ white (Swiss darning)

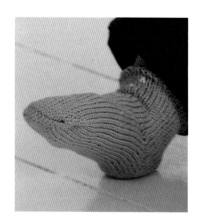

big ears

Big floppy ears adorn these jolly jumbo socks! The basic socks are
worked on four needles using a comfy wool and cotton yarn.
The elephant's head is knitted separately and sewn on afterwards.

materials

One 50g (1¾ oz) ball of Rowan Wool Cotton
in grey (Moonstone 961)
Small amount of same yarn in cream (Antique 900)
for tusks

extras

tiny wobbly toy eyes (or black beads)

tension/gauge

22 sts and 30 rows to 10 cm (4 in) measured over stocking
(stockinette) st using 4mm (US size 6) needles.

needles

Set of 4 double-pointed 4 mm (UK 8) (US size 6)
knitting needles
Pair of 4 mm (UK 8) (US size 6) knitting needles

sizes

to fit age 6–12 [12–18:18–24] mths
length of foot 9.5 [10:10.5] cm (3¾ [4:4¼] in)

abbreviations

K knit; M1 make one stitch knitways by picking up loop
between needles and knitting into back of this loop;
M1P make one stitch purlways by picking up loop between
needles and purling into back of this loop; P purl;
psso pass slipped stitch over; rem remaining; rep repeat;
RS right side; sl 1 slip one stitch; st(s) stitch(es);
tbl through back of loops; stocking (stockinette) st RS
rows K, WS rows P; tog together; 0 no stitches worked for
this size; g grams; oz ounces; mm millimetres;
mths months; cm centimetres; in inches.

52

big ears

Socks
(both alike)

Using double-pointed needles and grey, cast on 24 [26:28] sts.

Distribute these sts over 3 of the needles and, using 4th needle, work in rounds as follows:

round 1 (RS) *K1, P1, rep from * to end. Rep this round twice more.

round 4 Knit.

Last round forms stocking (stockinette) st. Work in stocking (stockinette) st for 16 rounds more.

Shape heel

row 1 (RS) K5 [5:6], wrap next st (by slipping next st from left needle onto right needle, taking yarn to opposite side of work between needles and then slipping same st back onto left needle – when working back across wrapped sts, work the wrapped st together with any wrapped loops) and turn.

Slip next 12 [13:14] sts of last complete round onto a spare needle and now working in rows, not rounds, work on rem set of 12 [13:14] sts only for heel as follows:

row 2 Sl 1, P9 [10:11], wrap next st and turn.

row 3 Sl 1, K8 [9:10], wrap next st and turn.

row 4 Sl 1, P7 [8:9], wrap next st and turn.

row 5 Sl 1, K6 [7:8], wrap next st and turn.

row 6 Sl 1, P5 [6:7], wrap next st and turn.

row 7 Sl 1, K4 [5:6], wrap next st and turn.

row 8 Sl 1, P3 [4:5], wrap next st and turn.

row 9 Rep row 7.

row 10 Rep row 6.

row 11 Rep row 5.

row 12 Rep row 4.

row 13 Rep row 3.

row 14 Rep row 2.

row 15 Sl 1, K10 [11:12], wrap next st and turn.

row 16 Sl 1, P11 [12:13], wrap next st (first stitch from spare needle) and turn.

row 17 Sl 1, K5 [6:6].

Distribute all 24 [26:28] sts over 3 needles and, using 4th needle, now work in rounds again and shape foot as follows:

Work 18 [20:22] rounds.

Shape toe

round 1 K4 [4:5], K2tog, sl 1, K1, psso, K8 [9:10], K2tog, sl 1, K1, psso, K4 [5:5]. 20 [22:24] sts.

round 2 Knit.

round 3 K3 [3:4], K2tog, sl 1, K1, psso, K6 [7:8], K2tog, sl 1, K1, psso, K3 [4:4]. 16 [18:20] sts.

round 4 Knit.

round 5 K2 [2:3], K2tog, sl 1, K1, psso, K4 [5:6], K2tog, sl 1, K1, psso, K2 [3:3]. 12 [14:16] sts.

round 6 K1 [1:2], K2tog, sl 1, K1, psso, K2 [3:4], K2tog, sl 1, K1, psso, K1 [2:2]. 8 [10:12] sts.

round 7 K2 [2:3].

Slip next 4 [5:6] sts onto one needle and rem 4 [5:6] sts onto another needle. Graft the 2 sets of 4 [5:6] sts together to close toe seam.

big ears

First elephant motif

First ear

Using pair of needles and grey, cast on 5 sts.
row 1 (RS) Knit.
row 2 K1, M1P, P3, M1P, K1. 7 sts.
row 3 Knit.
row 4 K1, M1P, P5, M1P, K1. 9 sts.
row 5 Knit.
row 6 K1, P7, M1P, K1. 10 sts.
row 7 Knit.
row 8 K1, P8, M1P, K1. 11 sts.
Break off yarn and leave sts on a holder.

Trunk and lower head

Using pair of needles grey, cast on 4 sts.**
row 1 (RS) K4.
row 2 K1, P2, K1.
row 3 K2, wrap next st and turn.
row 4 Sl 1, K1.
rows 5 to 16 (Rep rows 1 to 4) 3 times.
rows 17 to 22 (Rep rows 1 and 2) 3 times.
***row 23** K1, M1, K2, M1, K1. 6 sts
row 24 K1, M1P, P4, M1P, K1. 8 sts.
row 25 K1, M1, K6, M1, K1. 10 sts.
row 26 K1, P8, K1.
Break off yarn and leave sts on a holder.

Second ear

Work as given for First Ear to end of row 5.
row 6 K1, M1P, P7, K1. 10 sts.
row 7 Knit.
row 8 K1, M1P, P8, K1. 11 sts.

Join sections

row 1 (RS) Knit 11 sts of Second Ear, work
across 10 sts of Trunk and Lower Head as
follows: K1, M1, K8, M1, K1, then knit across
11 sts of First Ear. 34 sts.
row 2 K1, [P10, K1] 3 times.
row 3 Knit.
rows 4 and 5 Rep rows 2 and 3.

row 6 Rep row 2.

Shape top of second ear

Row 7 (RS) K11 and turn, leaving rem sts
on a holder.
Work on this set of 11 sts only for top of
Second Ear.
row 8 K2tog, P8, K1. 10 sts.
row 9 K2tog tbl, K6, K2tog. 8 sts.
row 10 K2tog, P5, K1. 7 sts.
row 11 K2tog tbl, K3, K2tog.
Cast (bind) off rem 5 sts.

Shape top of head

With RS facing, rejoin yarn to sts on holder
and shape top of Head as follows:
row 7 (RS) K2tog tbl, K8, K2tog and turn,
leaving rem sts on a holder.
Work on this set of 10 sts only for top
of Head.
row 8 K1, P8, K1.
row 9 K2tog tbl, K6, K2tog. 8 sts.
row 10 K2tog, P4, K2tog.
Cast (bind) off rem 6 sts.

Shape top of first ear

With RS facing, rejoin yarn to sts on
holder and shape top of First Ear as
follows:
row 7 (RS) K11.
row 8 K1, P8, K2tog. 10 sts.
row 9 K2tog tbl, K6, K2tog. 8 sts.
row 10 K1, P5, K2tog. 7 sts.
row 11 K2tog tbl, K3, K2tog.
Cast (bind) off rem 5 sts.

Second elephant motif

Work as given for First Elephant Motif to
**.
row 1 (RS) K4.
row 2 K1, P1, wrap next st and turn.

row 3 Sl 1, K1.
row 4 K1, P2, K1.
rows 5 to 16 (Rep rows 1 to 4) 3 times.
row 17 K4.
row 18 K1, P2, K1.
rows 19 to 22 (Rep rows 17 and 18)
twice.
Complete as given for First Elephant Motif
from ***.

Finishing

Press following instructions on yarn label.
Using photograph as a guide, sew elephant
motif to front of foot, leaving ears free.
(Ears are very floppy – just like the real
ones! If you wish to make them firmer,
attach a piece of matching felt to the back
of them.)
Sew on eyes. (*Note:* To avoid the eyes
coming off and being swallowed, ensure
they are very firmly attached. You may
prefer to embroider eyes using a scrap of
black yarn.)
Embroider tusks in cream, as in photograph.

fuzzy buzzy bee

Super easy to knit on two needles in garter stitch, these stripy
little socks use a mohair and a tweedy yarn together to create the fuzzy
buzzy bee look. Add some gauzy ribbon wings and baby is ready to buzz off!

materials

One 25 g (⅞ oz) ball of Rowan Scottish Tweed 4-Ply
in each of brown (Peat 019) and gold (Gold 028)
One 25 g (⅞ oz) ball of Rowan Kidsilk Haze in each of
black (Wicked 599) and orange (Marmalade 596)

extras

100 cm (39½ in) of 38 mm (1½ in) wide black organza
ribbon for wings and matching sewing thread

needles

Pair of 3.25 mm (UK 10) (US size 3) knitting needles

sizes

to fit age 6–12 [12–18:18–24] mths
length of foot 9.5 [10:10.5] cm (3¾ [4:4¼] in)

tension/gauge

26 sts and 38 rows to 10 cm (4 in) measured over garter st
using 3.25 mm (US size 3) needles.

special note

Two strands of yarn held together are used throughout –
one strand of Scottish Tweed 4-Ply and one strand
of Kidsilk Haze.

abbreviations

K knit; rem remaining; rep repeat; RS right side;
st(s) stitch(es); tbl through back of loops; tog together;
WS wrong side; g grams; oz ounces; mm millimetres;
mths months; cm centimetres; in inches.

fuzzy buzzy bee

Left sock

Using brown and black held together, cast on 28 [30:32] sts.

Work in garter st (K every row) for 10 [12:12] rows, ending with a WS row.

Join in gold and orange.

Using gold and orange held together, work 10 [10:12] rows in garter st.

Using brown and black held together, work 2 [2:4] rows, ending with a WS row.

Shape heel

Slip first 14 [15:16] sts of next row onto a spare needle, and last st onto a safety pin. Rejoin separate balls of brown and black held together to rem 13 [14:15] sts and work on these sts only for heel as follows: Work 8 rows, ending with a WS row.

row 9 (RS) K8 [9:10], K2tog tbl and turn.

row 10 K4 [5:6], K2tog and turn.

row 11 K4 [5:6], K2tog tbl and turn.

rows 12 to 15 (Rep rows 10 and 11) twice.

row 16 Rep row 10. 5 [6:7] sts.

Break off yarn.

Return to sts left on spare needle and, using brown and black held together, K 14 [15:16] sts from spare needle, pick up and knit 4 sts up first row-end edge of heel, K 5 [6:7] heel sts, pick up and knit 4 sts down second side of heel, then K st on safety pin. 28 [30:32] sts.

**Work in garter st using brown and black held together for 7 more rows, ending with a WS row.

Using gold and orange held together, work 10 [10:12] rows in garter st.

Break off gold and orange and complete sock using brown and black held together only.

Work 4 [6:6] rows, ending with a WS row.

Shape toe

row 1 K1, (K2tog, K9 [10:11], K2tog tbl) twice, K1. 24 [26:28] sts.

row 2 Knit.

row 3 K1, (K2tog, K7 [8:9], K2tog tbl) twice, K1. 20 [22:24] sts.

row 4 Knit.

row 5 K1, (K2tog, K5 [6:7], K2tog tbl) twice, K1. 16 [18:20] sts.

row 6 Knit.

Cast (bind) off.

Right sock

Work as given for Left Sock to start of heel shaping.

Shape heel

Slip *last* 14 [15:16] sts of next row onto a spare needle, and *first* st onto a safety pin. Rejoin separate balls of brown and black held together to rem 13 [14:15] sts and work on these sts only for heel as follows: Work 8 rows, ending with a WS row.

row 9 (RS) K8 [9:10], K2tog tbl and turn.

row 10 K4 [5:6], K2tog and turn.

row 11 K4 [5:6], K2tog tbl and turn.

rows 12 to 15 (Rep rows 10 and 11) twice.

row 16 Rep row 10. 5 [6:7] sts.

Break off yarn.

Return to sts left on spare needle and, using brown and black held together, K st on safety pin, pick up and knit 4 sts up first row-end edge of heel, K 5 [6:7] heel sts, pick up and knit 4 sts down second side of heel, then K 14 [15:16] sts from spare needle. 28 [30:32] sts.

Complete as given for Left Sock from **.

Finishing

Sew inside leg, foot and toe seams.

Do *not* press.

Cut ribbon into four equal lengths. Fold each length into a loop and run a gathering thread across centre of loop. Pull up tight and fasten off securely. Prepare each length of ribbon in the same way to form four pairs of wings. Sew two pairs of wings to heel of each sock as in photographs.

butterfly

These plain little socks, worked on four needles, are made really special
by adding a butterfly. One fluttering butterfly wing is on each sock
so that, when they are next to each other, they form a complete butterfly.

materials

One 50 g (1¾ oz) ball of Rowan 4-Ply Soft
in pale blue (Whisper 370)
One 25 g (⅞ oz) ball of Rowan Kidsilk Haze in each of
magenta (Splendour 579), jade (Trance 582)
and black (Wicked 599) (for butterfly)

needles

Set of 4 double-pointed 3.25 mm (UK 10) (US size 3)
knitting needles
Pair of 3.25 mm (UK 10) (US size 3) knitting needles

sizes

to fit age 18 mths–2 yrs [2–3 yrs:3–4 yrs]
length of foot 12.5 [13.5:14.5] cm (5 [5¼:5¾] in)

tension/gauge

28 sts and 36 rows to 10 cm (4 in) measured over stocking
(stockinette) st using 3.25 mm (US size 3) needles.

abbreviations

inc increase; K knit; P purl; psso pass slipped stitch over;
rem remaining; rep repeat; RS right side; sl 1 slip one stitch;
st(s) stitch(es); stocking (stockinette) st RS rows K, WS
rows P; tbl through back of loops; tog together;
WS wrong side; 0 no stitches worked for this size; g grams;
oz ounces; mm millimetres; mths months; yrs years;
cm centimetres; in inches.

butterfly

Socks
(both alike)

Using double-pointed needles and pale blue, cast on 36 [38:40] sts.

Distribute these sts over 3 of the needles and, using 4th needle, work in rounds as follows:

round 1 (RS) *K1, P1, rep from * to end. Rep this round 5 times more, inc 1 st at each end of last round. 38 [40:42] sts.

round 7 Knit.

This round forms stocking (stockinette) st. Work in stocking (stockinette) st for 15 rounds.

round 23 K1, sl 1, K1, psso, K to last 4 [3:4] sts, K2tog, K2 [1:2]. 36 [38:40] sts. Work in stocking (stockinette) st for 9 rounds.

round 33 Rep round 23. 34 [36:38] sts. Work 7 rounds.

Shape heel

row 1 (RS) K7 [8:8], wrap next st (by slipping next st from left needle onto right needle, taking yarn to opposite side of work between needles and then slipping same st back onto left needle – when working back across wrapped sts, work the wrapped st together with any wrapped loops) and turn.

Slip next 17 [18:19] sts of last complete round onto a spare needle and now working in rows, not rounds, work on rem set of

17 [18:19] sts only for heel as follows:

row 2 Sl 1, P14 [15:16], wrap next st and turn.

row 3 Sl 1, K13 [14:15], wrap next st and turn.

row 4 Sl 1, P12 [13:14], wrap next st and turn.

row 5 Sl 1, K11 [12:13], wrap next st and turn.

row 6 Sl 1, P10 [11:12], wrap next st and turn.

row 7 Sl 1, K9 [10:11], wrap next st and turn.

row 8 Sl 1, P8 [9:10], wrap next st and turn.

row 9 Rep row 7.

row 10 Rep row 6.

row 11 Rep row 5.

row 12 Rep row 4.

row 13 Rep row 3.

row 14 Rep row 2.

row 15 Sl 1, K15 [16:17], wrap next st and turn.

row 16 Sl 1, P16 [17:18], wrap next st (first stitch from spare needle) and turn.

row 17 Sl 1, K8 [8:9].

Distribute all 34 [36:38] sts over 3 needles

and, using 4th needle, now work in rounds again and shape foot as follows:
Work 34 [36:38] rounds.

Shape toe

round 1 K6 [7:7], K2tog, sl 1, K1, psso, K13 [14:15], K2tog, sl 1, K1, psso, K7 [7:8]. 30 [32:34] sts.

round 2 Knit.

round 3 K5 [6:6], K2tog, sl 1, K1, psso, K11 [12:13], K2tog, sl 1, K1, psso, K6 [6:7]. 26 [28:30] sts.

round 4 Knit.

round 5 K4 [5:5], K2tog, sl 1, K1, psso, K9 [10:11], K2tog, sl 1, K1, psso, K5 [5:6]. 22 [24:26] sts.

round 6 Knit.

round 7 K3 [4:4], K2tog, sl 1, K1, psso, K7 [8:9], K2tog, sl 1, K1, psso, K4 [4:5]. 18 [20:22] sts.

round 8 Knit.

round 9 K4 [5:5].
Slip next 9 [10:11] sts onto one needle and rem 9 [10:11] sts onto another needle. Graft the 2 sets of 9 [10:11] sts together to close toe seam.

Butterfly sections (make 2)

Upper wing

Using pair of needles and 2 strands of magenta held together, cast on 40 sts.

row 1 (RS) P1, (P2tog, P1) to end. 27 sts.

row 2 P19, wrap next st and turn.

row 3 Sl 1, K10, wrap next st and turn.

row 4 Sl 1, P to end.

rows 5 and 6 Knit.
Break off magenta and join in 2 strands of jade held together.

row 7 K6, K2tog, K3, K2tog, K1, K2tog tbl, K3, K2tog tbl, K6. 23 sts.

row 8 K5, K2tog, K2, K2tog, K1, K2tog tbl, K2, K2tog tbl, K5. 19 sts.

row 9 K4, (K2tog, K1) twice, K2tog tbl, K1, K2tog tbl, K4. 15 sts.

row 10 K3, (K2tog) twice, K1, (K2tog tbl) twice, K3. 11 sts.

row 11 K4, K2tog.
Fold Wing in half so that the 2 needles, each holding 5 sts, are together and, using a spare needle, cast (bind) off both sets of 5 sts together to form centre seam of Wing.

Lower wing

Using pair of needles and 2 strands of magenta held together, cast on 37 sts.

row 1 (RS) P1, (P2tog, P1) to end. 25 sts.

row 2 Purl.

rows 3 and 4 Knit.

row 5 K5, K2tog, K3, K2tog, K1, K2tog tbl, K3, K2tog tbl, K5. 21 sts.

row 6 K4, K2tog, K2, K2tog, K1, K2tog tbl, K2, K2tog tbl, K4. 17 sts.
Break off magenta and join in 2 strands of jade held together.

row 7 K3, (K2tog, K1) twice, K2tog tbl, K1, K2tog tbl, K3. 13 sts.

row 8 K2, (K2tog) twice, K1, (K2tog tbl) twice, K2. 9 sts.

row 9 K3, K2tog.
Fold Wing in half so that the 2 needles, each holding 4 sts, are together and, using a spare needle, cast (bind) off both sets of 4 sts together to form centre seam of Wing.

Body

Using pair of needles and 2 strands of black held together, cast on 2 sts, then using needle with 2 cast-on sts and with RS of Wings facing, pick up and knit 6 sts along row-end edge of one Wing (Lower Wing for right sock, or Upper Wing for left sock), then 6 sts along row-end edge of other Wing, cast on 2 sts onto same needle. 16 sts.

row 1 (WS) Inc in first st, K2, (K2tog) 5 times, K2, inc in last st. 13 sts.

row 2 Inc in first st, K to last st, inc in last st. 15 sts.

row 3 Rep row 2. 17 sts.

rows 4 and 5 Knit.

row 6 K2tog, K to last 2 sts, K2tog. 15 sts.

rows 7 and 8 Rep row 6. 11 sts.
Cast (bind) off knitwise (on WS).

Finishing

Press socks carefully following instructions on yarn label. Do *not* press butterfly section. Using photograph as a guide and leaving wings free, sew body sections of butterflies onto side leg sections of socks. Using black, embroider antennae onto socks by working a curved line of back-stitch with a French knot at the end. Socks can be worn so that body sections meet on inside of leg, to form a complete butterfly, or with butterflies on outside of leg, as though the butterfly had just settled.

snake socksss

Kids will love slithering their feet into these fun socks – and they make great glove puppets for older children, too! The socks are easy to work on two needles, and the tongues are knitted separately and stitched on.

materials

One 50 g (1¾ oz) ball of Rowan Wool Cotton
in each of dark green (Deepest Olive 907),
lime green (Citron 901) and mid green (Elf 946)
Small amount of same yarn in red (Rich 911)

needles

Pair of 3.25 mm (UK 10) (US size 3) knitting needles
Pair of 4 mm (UK 8) (US size 6) knitting needles

sizes

to fit age 18 mths–2 yrs [2–3 yrs:3–4 yrs]
length of foot 12.5 [13.5:14.5] cm (5 [5¼:5¾ in])

tension/gauge

22 sts and 30 rows to 10 cm (4 in) measured over reverse
stocking (stockinette) st using 4 mm (US size 6) needles.

abbreviations

cont continue; inc increase; K knit; P purl;
psso pass slipped stitch over; rem remaining; rep repeat;
reverse stocking (stockinette) st RS rows P, WS rows K;
RS right side; sl 1 slip one stitch; st(s) stitch(es);
tbl through back of loops; tog together; WS wrong side;
g grams; oz ounces; mm millimetres; mths months;
yrs years; cm centimetres; in inches.

Right sock

Using 3.25mm (US size 3) needles and dark green, cast on 31 [33:35] sts.

row 1 (RS) K1, *P1, K1, rep from * to end.

row 2 *P1, K1, rep from * to last st, inc in last st. 32 [34:36] sts.

Change to 4mm (US size 6) needles.

Now work in striped reverse stocking (stockinette) st as follows:

Join in lime green.

row 1 (RS) Using lime green, purl.

row 2 Using lime green, knit.

rows 3 and 4 Rep rows 1 and 2.

Join in mid green.

row 5 Using mid green, purl.

row 6 Using mid green, knit.

row 7 Using dark green, purl.

row 8 Using dark green, knit.

rows 9 and 10 Rep rows 7 and 8.

rows 11 and 12 Rep rows 1 and 2.

rows 13 to 16 (Rep rows 5 and 6) twice.

rows 17 and 18 Rep rows 7 and 8.

These 18 rows form striped reverse stocking (stockinette) st.

Cont as set for 6 [8:10] rows more, ending after 2 [2:4] rows using mid green [dark green:dark green] and with RS facing for next row.**

Keeping stripes correct, cont as follows:

next row (RS) P6 [7:8], P2tog tbl, P1, P2tog,

P to end. 30 [32:34] sts.

Work 7 rows.

next row (RS) P5 [6:7], P2tog tbl, P1, P2tog,

P to end. 28 [30:32] sts.

Work 3 [5:7] rows more, ending after 2 [4:2] rows using dark green [lime

snake socksss

green:dark green] and with RS facing for next row.

Shape heel
next row (RS) Using dark green, K14 [15:16] and turn, leaving rem 14 [15:16] sts on a holder.

Using dark green throughout, work on this set of sts *only* for heel as follows:
Starting with a P row, work in stocking (stockinette) st for 7 rows, ending with RS facing for next row.

next row (RS) K9 [10:11], sl 1, K1, psso and turn.

next row P5 [6:7], P2tog and turn.

next row K5 [6:7], sl 1, K1, psso and turn.

Rep last 2 rows twice more, then first of these rows again, ending with RS facing for next row. 6 [7:8] sts.

Break off yarn.

Shape foot
With RS facing and using lime green [mid green:dark green], pick up and knit 4 sts up first row-end edge of heel, knit 6 [7:8] heel sts, pick up and knit 4 sts down other row-end edge of heel, P to end. 28 [30:32] sts.

***Keeping stripes correct as set by leg section, work in striped reverse stocking (stockinette) st for 17 [19:21] rows, ending after 2 rows using dark green [mid green:lime green] and with RS facing for next row.

Break off mid green and lime green and cont using dark green only.

Shape toe
rows 1 and 2 Purl.

row 3 (RS) (K1, sl 1, K1, psso, K8 [9:10], K2tog, K1) twice. 24 [26:28] sts.

row 4 Purl.

row 5 (K1, sl 1, K1, psso, K6 [7:8], K2tog, K1) twice. 20 [22:24] sts.

row 6 Purl.

row 7 (K1, sl 1, K1, psso, K4 [5:6], K2tog, K1) twice. 16 [18:20] sts.

row 8 Purl.

Cast (bind) off.

Left sock
Work as given for Right Sock to **.
Keeping stripes correct, cont as follows:

next row (RS) P21 [22:23], P2tog tbl, P1, P2tog, P to end. 30 [32:34] sts.

Work 7 rows.

next row (RS) P20 [21:22], P2tog tbl, P1, P2tog, P to end. 28 [30:32] sts.

Work 3 [5:7] rows more, ending after 2 [4:2] rows using dark green [mid green:dark green] and with RS facing for next row.

Shape heel
next row (RS) Slip first 14 [15:16] sts onto a holder, rejoin dark green and using dark green K to end. 14 [15:16] sts.

Using dark green throughout, work on this set of sts *only* for heel as follows:
Starting with a P row, work in stocking (stockinette) st for 7 rows, ending with RS facing for next row.

next row (RS) K9 [10:11], sl 1, K1, psso and turn.

next row P5 [6:7], P2tog and turn.

next row K5 [6:7], sl 1, K1, psso and turn.

Rep last 2 rows twice more, then first of these rows again, ending with RS facing for next row. 6 [7:8] sts.

Break off yarn.

Shape foot
With RS facing and using lime green [mid green:dark green], purl across 14 [15:16] sts

left on holder, pick up and knit 4 sts up first row-end edge of heel, knit 6 [7:8] heel sts, pick up and knit 4 sts down other row-end edge of heel. 28 [30:32] sts.

Complete as given for Right Sock from ***.

Finishing
Press following instructions on yarn label.

Tongue
(make 1 for each sock)
Using 3.25mm (US size 3) needles and red, cast on 10 sts.

row 1 (WS) Cast (bind) off 4 sts knitwise, slip st on right needle back onto left needle, cast on 4 sts onto left needle (using knit cast-on), cast (bind) off all 10 sts knitwise.

Sew toe, foot and inside leg seams. Sew end of Tongue to centre of toe seam. Using red, embroider satin stitch eyes onto top of foot.

quack!

Go quackers and knit your little darling these clever socks shaped like duck feet! Quick to knit on four needles, the extra-wide foot leaves plenty of room for tiny toes to wriggle.

materials

One 50 g (1¾ oz) ball of Rowan Pure Wool DK in yellow (Gilt 032)

needles

Set of 4 double-pointed 4mm (UK 8) (US size 6) knitting needles

sizes

to fit age 0–3 [3–6:6–12:12–18] mths

length of foot 8.5 [9:9.5:10] cm (3¼ [3½:3¾:4] in)

tension/gauge

22 sts and 30 rows to 10 cm (4 in) measured over stocking (stockinette) st using 4 mm (US size 6) needles.

abbreviations

beg beginning; **inc** increase; **K** knit; **M1** make one stitch by picking up loop lying between needles and working into back of this loop; **P** purl; **psso** pass slipped stitch over; **rem** remaining; **rep** repeat; **RS** right side; **sl 1** slip one stitch; **st(s)** stitch(es); **stocking (stockinette) st** RS rows K, WS rows P; **tog** together; **0** no stitches worked for this size; **g** grams; **oz** ounces; **mm** millimetres; **mths** months; **cm** centimetres; **in** inches.

quack!

Socks
(both alike)
Cast on 22 [24:26:28] sts.
Distribute these sts over 3 of the needles
and, using 4th needle, work in rounds
as follows:
round 1 (RS) *K1, P1, rep from * to end.
Rep this round 11 times more.
round 13 Knit.
This round forms stocking (stockinette) st.
Work 1 more round.
Shape heel
row 1 (RS) K4 [5:5:6], wrap next st (by
slipping next st from left needle onto right
needle, taking yarn to opposite side of
work between needles and then slipping
same st back onto left needle – when
working back across wrapped sts, work the
wrapped st together with any wrapped
loops) and turn.
Slip next 11 [12:13:14] sts of last complete
round onto a spare needle and now working in rows, not rounds, work on rem set of
11 [12:13:14] sts only for heel as follows:
row 2 Sl 1, P8 [9:10:11], wrap next st
and turn.
row 3 Sl 1, K7 [8:9:10], wrap next st
and turn.
row 4 Sl 1, P6 [7:8:9], wrap next st and
turn.
row 5 Sl 1, K5 [6:7:8], wrap next st and
turn.
row 6 Sl 1, P4 [5:6:7], wrap next st and
turn.
row 7 Rep row 5.
row 8 Rep row 4.
row 9 Rep row 3.
row 10 Rep row 2.

row 11 Sl 1, K9 [10:11:12], wrap next st
and turn.
row 12 Sl 1, P10 [11:12:13], wrap next st
(first stitch from spare needle) and turn.
row 13 Sl 1, K5 [5:6:6].
Distribute all 22 [24:26:28] sts over 3
needles and, using 4th needle, now work
in rounds again and shape foot as follows:
Work 2 [2:3:3] rounds.
Counting from beg of last round place
marker on needle after 5th [6th:6th:7th] st
and counting from end of last round place
marker on needle after 6th [6th:7th:7th] st.
(There should be 11 [12:13:14] sts
between markers.)
next round *K to within 1 st of marker,
M1, K2 (marker is between these 2 sts),
M1, rep from * once more, K to end.
Work 2 rounds.
Rep last 3 rounds 3 times more, then first
of these rounds (the inc round) again.
Work 2 [3:3:4] rounds.

Shape toe
round 1 *K to within 2 sts of marker,
K2tog, slip marker onto right needle, sl 1,
K1, psso, rep from * once more, K to end.
round 2 *K to within 3 sts of marker,
K3tog, slip marker onto right needle, sl 1,
K2tog, psso, rep from * once more, K
to end.
Rep last 2 rows twice more, then first of
these 2 rounds 0 [0:1:1] times more.
next round K1 [2:1:2].
Slip next 3 [4:3:4] sts onto one needle and
rem 3 [4:3:4] sts onto another needle.
Graft the 2 sets of 3 [4:3:4] sts together to
close toe seam.

Finishing
Press carefully following instructions on
yarn label.
If you want the sock shape to be more
rigid, apply heavy-weight iron-on interfacing
to sole inside each sock.

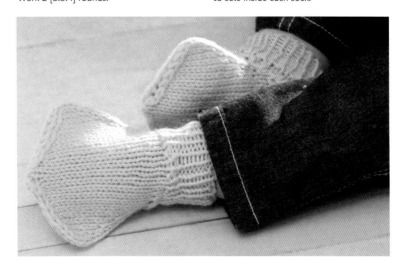

zebra feet

Let your little one walk on the wild side in these clever zebra
striped socks knitted on four needles in a luxurious soft yarn.
Why not knit a second pair in gold and brown to turn him into a tiny tiger?

materials

One 50 g (1¾ oz) ball of Rowan RYC Cashsoft 4-Ply
in each of black (Black 422) and cream (Cream 433)

needles

Set of 4 double-pointed 3.25 mm (UK 10) (US size 3)
knitting needles

sizes

to fit age 0–3 [3–6:6–12:12–18] mths
length of foot 8.5 [9:9.5:10] cm (3¼ [3½:3¾:4] in)

tension/gauge

28 sts and 36 rows to 10 cm (4 in) measured over stocking
(stockinette) st using 3.25 mm (US size 3) needles.

abbreviations

K knit; P purl; psso pass slipped stitch over;
rem remaining; rep repeat; RS right side; sl 1 slip one stitch;
st(s) stitch(es); stocking (stockinette) st RS rows K, WS
rows P; tog together; WS wrong side; g grams;
oz ounces; mm millimetres; mths months;
cm centimetres; in inches.

zebra feet

Socks
(both alike)

Using black, cast on 28 [30:32:34] sts.
Distribute these sts over 3 of the needles
and, using 4th needle, work in rounds as
follows:

round 1 (RS) *K1, P1, rep from * to end.
Rep this round 3 times more.

Join in cream.

Starting and ending rounds as indicated
and stranding yarn not in use loosely
across WS of work, weaving it in every 3
or 4 sts, now work in rounds of stocking
(stockinette) st (knit every round)
following chart as follows:

(*Note*: For first sock read every row of
chart from right to left. For second sock
read every row of chart from left to right to
reverse design and make a pair of socks.)
Work 24 rounds.

Shape heel

row 1 (RS) Using black, K6 [7:7:8], wrap
next st (by slipping next st from left needle
onto right needle, taking yarn to opposite
side of work between needles and then
slipping same st back onto left needle –
when working back across wrapped sts,
work the wrapped st together with any
wrapped loops) and turn.

Slip next 14 [15:16:17] sts of last complete
round onto a spare needle and now
working in rows, not rounds, work on rem
set of 14 [15:16:17] sts only for heel using
black *only* as follows:

row 2 Sl 1, P11 [12:13:14], wrap next st
and turn.

row 3 Sl 1, K10 [11:12:13], wrap next st
and turn.

zebra feet

row 4 Sl 1, P9 [10:11:12], wrap next st and turn.

row 5 Sl 1, K8 [9:10:11], wrap next st and turn.

row 6 Sl 1, P7 [8:9:10], wrap next st and turn.

row 7 Sl 1, K6 [7:8:9], wrap next st and turn.

row 8 Sl 1, P5 [6:7:8], wrap next st and turn.

row 9 Rep row 7.

row 10 Rep row 6.

row 11 Rep row 5.

row 12 Rep row 4.

row 13 Rep row 3.

row 14 Rep row 2.

row 15 Sl 1, K12 [13:14:15], wrap next st and turn.

row 16 Sl 1, P13 [14:15:16], wrap next st (first stitch from spare needle) and turn.

row 17 Sl 1, K6 [6:7:7].

Distribute all 28 [30:32:34] sts over 3 needles and, using 4th needle, now work in rounds again and shape foot as follows: Starting with row 25 of chart, work 18 [20:22:24] rounds.

Shape toe

Break off cream and complete sock using black *only*.

rounds 1 and 2 Knit.

round 3 K5 [6:6:7], K2tog, sl 1, K1, psso, K10 [11:12:13], K2tog, sl 1, K1, psso, K5 [5:6:6].

round 4 Knit.

round 5 K4 [5:5:6], K2tog, sl 1, K1, psso, K8 [9:10:11], K2tog, sl 1, K1, psso, K4 [4:5:5].

round 6 Knit.

round 7 K3 [4:4:5], K2tog, sl 1, K1, psso, K6 [7:8:9], K2tog, sl 1, K1, psso, K3 [3:4:4].

round 8 Knit.

round 9 K4 [5:5:6].

Slip next 8 [9:10:11] sts onto one needle and rem 8 [9:10:11] sts onto another needle. Graft the 2 sets of 8 [9:10:11] sts together to close toe seam.

Finishing

Press carefully following instructions on yarn label.

Key
■ black
□ cream

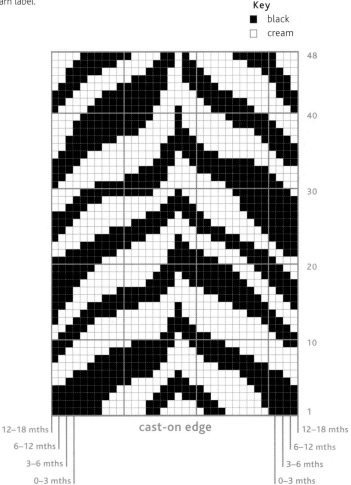

cast-on edge

12–18 mths
6–12 mths
3–6 mths
0–3 mths

12–18 mths
6–12 mths
3–6 mths
0–3 mths

bright and bold

beautiful balloons

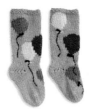

He'll be flying high in these snug socks decorated with bright balloons!
Worked in a pure wool yarn on four needles, they are quick and easy
to knit because the balloons are embroidered on afterwards.

materials
One 50 g (1¾ oz) ball of Rowan Pure Wool DK
in blue (Pier 006)
Small amount of same yarn in yellow (Gilt 032),
red (Scarlet 041), orange (Tangerine 040),
and black (Black 004) for embroidery

needles
Set of 4 double-pointed 4 mm (UK 8) (US size 6)
knitting needles

sizes
to fit age 18 mths–2 yrs [2–3 yrs:3–4 yrs]
length of foot 12.5 [13.5:14.5] cm (5 [5¼:5¾] in)

tension/gauge
22 sts and 30 rows to 10 cm (4 in) measured over stocking
(stockinette) st using 4 mm (US size 6) needles.

abbreviations
K knit; P purl; psso pass slipped stitch over; rem remaining;
rep repeat; RS right side; sl 1 slip one stitch; st(s) stitch(es);
stocking (stockinette) st RS rows K, WS rows P;
tog together; 0 no stitches worked for this size; g grams;
oz ounces; mm millimetres; mths months; yrs years;
cm centimetres; in inches.

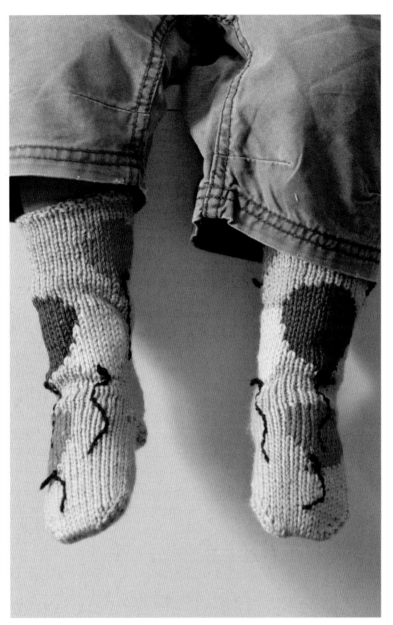

Socks
(both alike)
Using blue, cast on 34 [36:38] sts.
Distribute these sts over 3 of the needles
and, using 4th needle, work in rounds
as follows:

round 1 (RS) *K1, P1, rep from * to end.

round 2 *P1, K1, rep from * to end.

round 3 Rep round 1.

round 4 Knit.

Last round forms stocking (stockinette) st.
Work in stocking (stockinette) st for
27 rounds.

round 32 Sl 1, K1, psso, K to last 3 [2:3]
sts, K2tog, K1 [0:1]. 32 [34:36] sts.
Work in stocking (stockinette) st for
9 rounds.

round 42 Rep round 32. 30 [32:34] sts.
Work 8 rounds.

Shape heel

row 1 (RS) K6 [7:7], wrap next st (by
slipping next st from left needle onto right
needle, taking yarn to opposite side of
work between needles and then slipping
same st back onto left needle – when
working back across wrapped sts, work the
wrapped st together with any wrapped
loops) and turn.

Slip next 15 [16:17] sts of last complete
round onto a spare needle and now working in rows, not rounds, work on rem set of
15 [16:17] sts only for heel as follows:

row 2 Sl 1, P12 [13:14], wrap next st
and turn.

row 3 Sl 1, K11 [12:13], wrap next st
and turn.

row 4 Sl 1, P10 [11:12], wrap next st
and turn.

row 5 Sl 1, K9 [10:11], wrap next st and turn.

row 6 Sl 1, P8 [9:10], wrap next st and turn.

row 7 Sl 1, K7 [8:9], wrap next st and turn.

row 8 Sl 1, P6 [7:8], wrap next st and turn.

row 9 Rep row 7.

row 10 Rep row 6.

row 11 Rep row 5.

row 12 Rep row 4.

row 13 Rep row 3.

row 14 Rep row 2.

row 15 Sl 1, K13 [14:15], wrap next st and turn.

row 16 Sl 1, P14 [15:16], wrap next st (first stitch from spare needle) and turn.

row 17 Sl 1, K7 [7:8].

Distribute all 30 [32:34] sts over 3 needles and, using 4th needle, now work in rounds again and shape foot as follows:

Work in stocking (stockinette) st for 20 [22:24] rounds.

Shape toe

round 1 K5 [6:6], K2tog, sl 1, K1, psso, K11 [12:13], K2tog, sl 1, K1, psso, K6 [6:7]. 26 [28:30] sts.

round 2 Knit.

round 3 K4 [5:5], K2tog, sl 1, K1, psso, K9 [10:11], K2tog, sl 1, K1, psso, K5 [5:6]. 22 [24:26] sts.

round 4 Knit.

round 5 K3 [4:4], K2tog, sl 1, K1, psso, K7 [8:9], K2tog, sl 1, K1, psso, K4 [4:5]. 18 [20:22] sts.

round 6 Knit.

round 7 K4 [5:5].

Slip next 9 [10:11] sts onto one needle and rem 9 [10:11] sts onto another needle.

Graft the 2 sets of 9 [10:11] sts together to close toe seam.

Finishing

Following chart, Swiss darn (duplicate stitch) balloons onto socks – place chart centrally on front of leg and foot starting 5 rounds down from cast-on edge and reversing chart for second sock (to make a pair). Using photograph as a guide and a length of black, knot this length of yarn around single stitch near base of balloon. Trim one end to approximately 1 cm (³⁄₈ in) and then, using other end, embroider a wavy line of backstitch for balloon string.

Press carefully following instructions on yarn label.

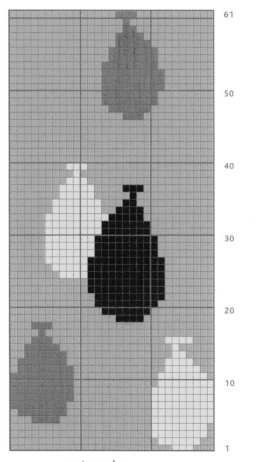

	Key
	blue
	yellow
	orange
	red

cast-on edge

flower power

Decorated with pretty flowers, these simple socks are worked up quickly on four needles. Knitted on two needles, the flowers are so easy that you could make a whole bouquet and sew them on around the tops.

materials

One 50 g (1¾ oz) ball of Rowan Pure Wool DK
in each of **dark pink** (Hyacinth 026)
and **light pink** (Tea Rose 025)
Small amount of same yarn in **yellow** (Gilt 032)
for flower centres

needles

Set of 4 double-pointed 4mm (UK 8) (US size 6)
knitting needles
Pair of 4 mm (UK 8) (US size 6) knitting needles

sizes

to fit age 18 mths–2 yrs [2–3 yrs:3–4 yrs]
length of foot 12.5 [13.5:14.5] cm (5 [5¼:5¾] in)

tension/gauge

22 sts and 30 rows to 10 cm (4 in) measured over stocking
(stockinette) st using 4 mm (US size 6) needles.

abbreviations

K knit; **P** purl; **psso** pass slipped stitch over; **rem** remaining;
rep repeat; **RS** right side; **sl 1** slip one stitch; **st(s)** stitch(es);
stocking (stockinette) st RS rows K, WS rows P; **tog** together; **yfwd** yarn forward – bring yarn forward between
needles and over right needle to make a new stitch (US
yarn over); **0** no stitches worked for this size;
g grams; **oz** ounces; **mm** millimetres; **mths** months;
yrs years; **cm** centimetres; **in** inches.

Right sock

Using set of double-pointed needles and dark pink, cast on 32 [34:36] sts.

Distribute these sts over 3 of the needles and, using 4th needle, work in rounds as follows:

round 1 (RS) *K1, P1, rep from * to end. Rep this round 3 times more.

round 5 Knit.

Last round forms stocking (stockinette) st. Work in stocking (stockinette) st for 21 rounds.

round 27 K7 [7:8], K2tog, K0 [1:0], sl 1, K1, psso, K to end. 30 [32:34] sts.

Work in stocking (stockinette) st for 7 rounds.

round 35 K6 [6:7], K2tog, K0 [1:0], sl 1, K1, psso, K to end. 28 [30:32] sts.

Work 5 rounds.

Shape heel

Slip last 14 [15:16] sts of last complete round onto a spare needle.

**Join in light pink.

Using light pink and now working in rows, not rounds, work on rem set of 14 [15:16] sts only for heel as follows:

row 1 (RS) K14 [15:16].

row 2 Sl 1, P12 [13:14], wrap next st (by slipping next st from left needle onto right needle, taking yarn to opposite side of work between needles and then slipping same st back onto left needle – when working back across wrapped sts, work the wrapped st together with any wrapped loops) and turn.

row 3 Sl 1, K11 [12:13], wrap next st and turn.

row 4 Sl 1, P10 [11:12], wrap next st and turn.

row 5 Sl 1, K9 [10:11], wrap next st and turn.

row 6 Sl 1, P8 [9:10], wrap next st and turn.

row 7 Sl 1, K7 [8:9], wrap next st and turn.

row 8 Sl 1, P6 [7:8], wrap next st and turn.

row 9 Rep row 7.

row 10 Rep row 6.

row 11 Rep row 5.

row 12 Rep row 4.

row 13 Rep row 3.

row 14 Rep row 2.

row 15 Sl 1, K13 [14:15], wrap next st (first stitch from spare needle) and turn.

row 16 Sl 1, P14 [15:16] and turn.

Break off light pink.

Distribute all 28 [30:32] sts over 3 needles and, using 4th needle, now work in rounds again using dark pink and shape foot as follows:

Work in stocking (stockinette) st for 20 [22:24] rounds.

Shape toe

Break off dark pink and join in light pink.

round 1 Knit.

round 2 (Sl 1, K1, psso, K10 [11:12], K2tog) twice. 24 [26:28] sts.

round 3 Knit.

round 4 (Sl 1, K1, psso, K8 [9:10], K2tog) twice. 20 [22:24] sts.

round 5 Knit.

round 6 (Sl 1, K1, psso, K6 [7:8], K2tog) twice. 16 [18:20] sts.

round 7 Knit.

round 8 (Sl 1, K1, psso, K4 [5:6], K2tog) twice. 12 [14:16] sts.

Slip first 6 [7:8] sts onto one needle and last 6 [7:8] sts onto another needle. Graft the 2 sets of 6 [7:8] sts together to close toe seam.

Left sock

Work as given for Right Sock to round 27.

round 27 K21 [22:24], K2tog, K0 [1:0], sl 1, K1, psso, K to end. 30 [32:34] sts.

Work in stocking (stockinette) st for 7 rounds.

round 35 K20 [21:23], K2tog, K0 [1:0], sl 1, K1, psso, K to end. 28 [30:32] sts.

Work 5 rounds.

Shape heel

Slip *first* 14 [15:16] sts of last complete round onto a spare needle.

Complete as given for Right Sock from **.

Flowers (make 2)

Using pair of needles and light pink, cast on 43 sts.

row 1 (RS) K1, *yfwd, K5, lift 2nd, 3rd, 4th and 5th sts on right needle over first st and off right needle, yfwd, K1, rep from * to end. 29 sts.

row 2 P1, *P3tog, P1, rep from * to end. 15 sts.

row 3 K1, (K2tog) 7 times.

Break off yarn and thread through rem 8 sts. Pull up tight and fasten off securely. Sew together row-end edges of Flower.

Flower centres (make 2)

Using pair of needles and yellow, cast on one st.

row 1 (RS) K into front, back, front, back and front again. 5 sts.

row 2 P5.

row 3 K5.

row 4 P5.

row 5 K2tog, K1, K2tog. 3 sts.

row 6 P3tog and fasten off.

Run a gathering thread around outer edge of Flower Centre and pull up to form a bobble. Fasten off securely.

Finishing

Using photograph as a guide, sew Flowers to sides of socks, attaching Flower Centres at centre.

Press carefully following instructions on yarn label.

dotty socks

You'll definitely be seeing spots before your eyes with these bright little socks! Knitted on four needles in bright, contrasting shades of cotton, the dots are embroidered on after the sock has been knitted.

materials

One 50 g (1¾ oz) ball of Rowan Cotton Glace in each of yellow (Buttercup 825), red (Poppy 741), purple (Excite 815) and green (Shoot 814)

needles

Set of 4 double-pointed 3.25 mm (UK 10) (US size 3) knitting needles

sizes

to fit age 6–12 [12–18:18–24] mths
length of foot 9.5 [10:10.5] cm (3¾ [4:4¼] in)

tension/gauge

23 sts and 32 rows to 10 cm (4 in) measured over stocking (stockinette) st using 3.25 mm (US size 3) needles.

abbreviations

K knit; P purl; psso pass slipped stitch over; rem remaining; rep repeat; RS right side; sl 1 slip one stitch; st(s) stitch(es); stocking (stockinette) st RS rows K, WS rows P; tog together; 0 no stitches worked for this size; g grams; oz ounces; mm millimetres; mths months; cm centimetres; in inches.

dotty socks

Right sock

Using red, cast on 26 [28:30] sts.
Distribute these sts over 3 of the needles and, using 4th needle, work in rounds as follows:

round 1 (RS) *K1, P1, rep from * to end.
Rep this round 13 times more.
Break off red and join in yellow.

round 15 Knit.
Last round forms stocking (stockinette) st.
Work in stocking (stockinette) st for 11 rounds.

Shape heel

Slip last 13 [14:15] sts of last round onto a spare needle.
**Join in purple.
Using purple and now working in rows, not rounds, work on rem set of 13 [14:15] sts only for heel as follows:

row 1 (RS) K13 [14:15].

row 2 Sl 1, P11 [12:13], wrap next st (by slipping next st from left needle onto right needle, taking yarn to opposite side of work between needles and then slipping same st back onto left needle – when working back across wrapped sts, work the wrapped st together with any wrapped loops) and turn.

row 3 Sl 1, K10 [11:12], wrap next st and turn.

row 4 Sl 1, P9 [10:11], wrap next st and turn.

row 5 Sl 1, K8 [9:10], wrap next st and turn.

row 6 Sl 1, P7 [8:9], wrap next st and turn.

row 7 Sl 1, K6 [7:8], wrap next st and turn.

row 8 Sl 1, P5 [6:7], wrap next st and turn.

row 9 Sl 1, K4 [5:6], wrap next st and turn.

row 10 Rep row 8.

row 11 Rep row 7.

row 12 Rep row 6.

row 13 Rep row 5.

row 14 Rep row 4.

row 15 Rep row 3.

row 16 Sl 1, P11 [12:13] and turn.
Break off purple.
Distribute all 26 [28:30] sts over 3 needles and, using 4th needle, now work in rounds again using yellow and shape foot as follows:
Work in stocking (stockinette) st for 22 [24:26] rounds.

Shape toe

Break off yellow and join in green.

round 1 Knit.

round 2 (Sl 1, K1, psso, K9 [10:11], K2tog) twice. 22 [24:26] sts.

round 3 Knit.

round 4 (Sl 1, K1, psso, K7 [8:9], K2tog) twice. 18 [20:22] sts.

round 5 Knit.

round 6 (Sl 1, K1, psso, K5 [6:7], K2tog) twice. 14 [16:18] sts.

round 7 Knit.
Slip first 7 [8:9] sts onto one needle and last 7 [8:9] sts onto another needle. Graft the 2 sets of 7 [8:9] sts together to close toe seam.

Left sock

Work as given for Right Sock to start of heel shaping.

Shape heel

Slip *first* 13 [14:15] sts of last complete round onto a spare needle.
Complete as given for Right Sock from **.

Finishing

Following chart, Swiss darn (duplicate stitch) dots onto socks – place chart centrally on front of sock starting 4 rounds down from first row in yellow and reversing position of colours for second sock (to make a pair).
Press carefully following instructions on yarn label.

cast-on edge

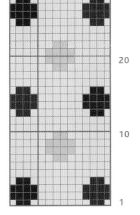

20

10

1

Key

☐ yellow
■ red (Swiss darning)
■ purple (Swiss darning)
☐ green (Swiss darning)

queen of hearts

Worked on four needles in a soft yarn, these neat little socks are crowned with a pretty picot edging – sure to make your little princess feel really royal! The heart motifs are embroidered on to the finished socks.

materials

One 50 g (1¾ oz) ball of Rowan RYC Cashsoft 4-Ply in red (Poppy 438)
Small amount of same yarn in cream (Cream 433) for embroidery

needles

Set of 4 double-pointed 3.25 mm (UK 10) (US size 3) knitting needles

sizes

to fit age 0–3 [3–6:6–12:12–18] mths
length of foot 8.5 [9:9.5:10] cm (3¼ [3½:3¾:4] in)

tension/gauge

28 sts and 36 rows to 10 cm (4 in) measured over stocking (stockinette) st using 3.25 mm (US size 3) needles.

abbreviations

K knit; P purl; psso pass slipped stitch over; rem remaining; rep repeat; RS right side; sl 1 slip one stitch; st(s) stitch(es); stocking (stockinette) st RS rows K, WS rows P; tog together; yfwd yarn forward – bring yarn forward between needles and over right needle to make a new stitch (US yarn over); 0 no stitches worked for this size; g grams; oz ounces; mm millimetres; mths months; cm centimetres; in inches.

queen of hearts

Socks

(both alike)

Using red, cast on 32 [34:36:38] sts.
Distribute these sts over 3 of the needles
and, using 4th needle, work in rounds as
follows:

round 1 (RS) Knit.
This round forms stocking (stockinette) st.
Work in stocking (stockinette) st for 2
rounds.

round 4 *Yfwd, K2tog, rep from * to end.
Work in stocking (stockinette) st for 3
rounds.

round 8 Fold cast-on edge to inside
and K tog first st of next round with
corresponding st of cast-on edge, *K tog
next st with corresponding st of cast-on
edge, rep from * to end.
This completes the picot border.
Work in stocking (stockinette) st for 9
[10:11:12] rounds.

next round K1, sl 1, K1, psso, K to last 2
[3:2:3] sts, K2tog, K0 [1:0:1]. 30 [32:34:36]
sts.
Work 7 rounds.

next round K1, sl 1, K1, psso, K to last 2
[3:2:3] sts, K2tog, K0 [1:0:1]. 28 [30:32:34]
sts.
Work 5 rounds.

Shape heel

row 1 (RS) K6 [7:7:8], wrap next st (by
slipping next st from left needle onto right
needle, taking yarn to opposite side of work
between needles and then slipping same st
back onto left needle — when working back
across wrapped sts, work the wrapped st
together with any wrapped loops) and turn.
Slip next 14 [15:16:17] sts of last complete

round onto a spare needle and now working in rows, not rounds, work on rem set of
14 [15:16:17] sts only for heel as follows:

row 2 Sl 1, P11 [12:13:14], wrap next st
and turn.

row 3 Sl 1, K10 [11:12:13], wrap next st
and turn.

row 4 Sl 1, P9 [10:11:12], wrap next st
and turn.

row 5 Sl 1, K8 [9:10:11], wrap next st and
turn.

row 6 Sl 1, P7 [8:9:10], wrap next st and
turn.

row 7 Sl 1, K6 [7:8:9], wrap next st and
turn.

row 8 Sl 1, P5 [6:7:8], wrap next st and
turn.

row 9 Rep row 7.

row 10 Rep row 6.

row 11 Rep row 5.

row 12 Rep row 4.

row 13 Rep row 3.

row 14 Rep row 2.

row 15 Sl 1, K12 [13:14:15], wrap next st
and turn.

row 16 Sl 1, P13 [14:15:16], wrap next st
(first stitch from spare needle) and turn.

row 17 Sl 1, K6 [6:7:7].
Distribute all 28 [30:32:34] sts over 3
needles and, using 4th needle, now work in
rounds again and shape foot as follows:

cast-on edge

Key
- ■ red
- □ cream (Swiss darning)

Work in stocking (stockinette) st for 20
[22:24:26] rounds.

Shape toe

round 1 K5 [6:6:7], K2tog, sl 1, K1, psso,
K10 [11:12:13], K2tog, sl 1, K1, psso, K5
[5:6:6]. 24 [26:28:30] sts.

round 2 Knit.

round 3 K4 [5:5:6], K2tog, sl 1, K1, psso, K8
[9:10:11], K2tog, sl 1, K1, psso, K4 [4:5:5].
20 [22:24:26] sts.

round 4 Knit.

round 5 K3 [4:4:5], K2tog, sl 1, K1, psso, K6
[7:8:9], K2tog, sl 1, K1, psso, K3 [3:4:4]. 16
[18:20:22] sts.

round 6 Knit.

round 7 K4 [5:5:6].
Slip next 8 [9:10:11] sts onto one needle
and rem 8 [9:10:11] sts onto another
needle. Graft the 2 sets of 8 [9:10:11] sts
together to close toe seam.

Finishing

Following chart, Swiss darn (duplicate
stitch) heart motifs onto socks using
cream — place one motif centrally on
top of foot starting 4 rounds after heel
shaping. Leave 10 rounds free above this
motif, then place ankle motifs so that
there are 7 sts left free at centre front.
Press carefully following instructions on
yarn label.

wizard socks

Make him feel like a true superstar in these jolly star-spangled socks!
They knit up quickly on four needles. And, as the little gold stars are
embroidered on afterwards, you can add as many or as few as you want.

materials

One 50 g (1¾ oz) ball of Rowan Pure Wool DK
in blue (Marine 008)
Small amount of same yarn in gold (Honey 033)
for embroidery

needles

Set of 4 double-pointed 4 mm (UK 8) (US size 6)
knitting needles

sizes

to fit age 18 mths–2 yrs [2–3 yrs:3–4 yrs]
length of foot 12.5 [13.5:14.5] cm (5 [5¼:5¾] in)

tension/gauge

22 sts and 30 rows to 10 cm (4 in) measured over stocking
(stockinette) st using 4 mm (US size 6) needles.

abbreviations

K knit; P purl; psso pass slipped stitch over; rem remaining;
rep repeat; RS right side; sl 1 slip one stitch; st(s) stitch(es);
stocking (stockinette) st RS rows K, WS rows P;
tog together; 0 no stitches worked for this size; g grams;
oz ounces; mm millimetres; mths months; yrs years;
cm centimetres; in inches.

wizard socks

Socks

(both alike)

Using blue, cast on 32 [34:36] sts. Distribute these sts over 3 of the needles and, using 4th needle, work in rounds as follows:

round 1 (RS) Knit.

This round forms stocking (stockinette) st. Work in stocking (stockinette) st for 3 rounds.

round 5 Purl.

This round forms a ridge that helps hold the roll around the top of the socks in place.

Work in stocking (stockinette) st for 18 rounds.

round 24 Sl 1, K1, psso, K to last 2 [3:2] sts, K2tog, K0 [1:0]. 30 [32:34] sts.

Work in stocking (stockinette) st for 9 rounds.

round 34 Rep round 24. 28 [30:32] sts.

Work 6 rounds.

Shape heel

row 1 (RS) K6 [6:7], wrap next st (by slipping next st from left needle onto right needle, taking yarn to opposite side of work between needles and then slipping same st back onto left needle — when working back across wrapped sts, work the wrapped st together with any wrapped loops) and turn.

Slip next 14 [15:16] sts of last complete round onto a spare needle and now working in rows, not rounds, work on rem set of 14 [15:16] sts only for heel as follows:

row 2 Sl 1, P11 [12:13], wrap next st and turn.

row 3 Sl 1, K10 [11:12], wrap next st and turn.

row 4 Sl 1, P9 [10:11], wrap next st and turn.

row 5 Sl 1, K8 [9:10], wrap next st and turn.

row 6 Sl 1, P7 [8:9], wrap next st and turn.

row 7 Sl 1, K6 [7:8], wrap next st and turn.

row 8 Sl 1, P5 [6:7], wrap next st and turn.

row 9 Rep row 7.

row 10 Rep row 6.

row 11 Rep row 5.

row 12 Rep row 4.

row 13 Rep row 3.

row 14 Rep row 2.

row 15 Sl 1, K12 [13:14], wrap next st and turn.

row 16 Sl 1, P13 [14:15], wrap next st (first stitch from spare needle) and turn.

row 17 Sl 1, K6 [7:7].

Distribute all 28 [30:32] sts over 3 needles and, using 4th needle, now work in rounds again and shape foot as follows:

Work 22 [24:26] rounds.

Shape toe

round 1 K5 [5:6], K2tog, sl 1, K1, psso, K10 [11:12], K2tog, sl 1, K1, psso, K5 [6:6]. 24 [26:28] sts.

round 2 Knit.

round 3 K4 [4:5], K2tog, sl 1, K1, psso, K8 [9:10], K2tog, sl 1, K1, psso, K4 [5:5]. 20 [22:24] sts.

round 4 Knit.

round 5 K3 [3:4], K2tog, sl 1, K1, psso, K6 [7:8], K2tog, sl 1, K1, psso, K3 [4:4]. 16 [18:20] sts.

round 6 Knit.

round 7 K4 [4:5].

Slip next 8 [9:10] sts onto one needle and rem 8 [9:10] sts onto another needle. Graft the 2 sets of 8 [9:10] sts together to close toe seam.

Finishing

Cut a length of gold yarn approximately 45 cm (18 in) long and carefully split this into two pairs of two strands — as if separating the strands of stranded embroidery thread (floss). Using photographs as a guide and these thin strands, embroider 5-pointed straight stitch stars at random over both socks. (If you prefer, use a fine gold yarn rather than splitting this thicker yarn.) Press carefully following instructions on yarn label.

fab fair isle

Knitted on four needles in a pure wool yarn, these Fair Isle socks are surprisingly easy to knit! There are only ever two colours used in a round, and lots of rounds use only one colour.

materials

One 25 g (⁷⁄₈ oz) ball of Rowan Scottish Tweed 4-Ply in each of cream (Porridge 024), green (Apple 015) and lilac (Lavender 005)

needles

Set of 4 double-pointed 3.25 mm (UK 10) (US size 3) knitting needles

sizes

to fit age 6–12 [12–18:18–24] mths
length of foot 9.5 [10:10.5] cm (3³⁄₄ [4:4¹⁄₄] in)

tension/gauge

26 sts and 36 rows to 10 cm (4 in) measured over Fair Isle pattern using 3.25 mm (US size 3) needles.

abbreviations

K knit; P purl; psso pass slipped stitch over; rem remaining; rep repeat; RS right side; sl 1 slip one stitch; st(s) stitch(es); stocking (stockinette) st RS rows K, WS rows P; tog together; WS wrong side; 0 no stitches worked for this size; g grams; oz ounces; mm millimetres; mths months; cm centimetres; in inches.

Right sock

Using cream, cast on 28 [30:32] sts. Distribute these sts over 3 of the needles and, using 4th needle, work in rounds as follows:

round 1 (RS) *K1, P1, rep from * to end. Rep this round 3 times more.

Join in green and lilac when required, starting and ending rounds as indicated and stranding yarn not in use loosely across WS of work, weaving it in every 3 or 4 sts, now work in rounds of stocking (stockinette) st (knit every round) following chart as follows:

Work 24 rounds.

Shape heel

row 1 (RS) Using cream, K13 [14:15], wrap next st (by slipping next st from left needle onto right needle, taking yarn to opposite side of work between needles and then slipping same st back onto left needle – when working back across wrapped sts, work the wrapped st together with any wrapped loops) and turn.

Slip next 14 [15:16] sts of last complete round onto a spare needle and now working in rows, not rounds, work on rem set of 14 [15:16] sts only for heel using cream *only* as follows:

row 2 Sl 1, P11 [12:13], wrap next st and turn.

row 3 Sl 1, K10 [11:12], wrap next st and turn.

row 4 Sl 1, P9 [10:11], wrap next st and turn.

row 5 Sl 1, K8 [9:10], wrap next st and turn.

row 6 Sl 1, P7 [8:9], wrap next st and turn.

row 7 Sl 1, K6 [7:8], wrap next st and turn.

row 8 Sl 1, P5 [6:7], wrap next st and turn.

row 9 Rep row 7.

row 10 Rep row 6.

row 11 Rep row 5.

row 12 Rep row 4.

row 13 Rep row 3.

row 14 Rep row 2.

row 15 Sl 1, K12 [13:14], wrap next st and turn.

row 16 Sl 1, P13 [14:15], wrap next st (first stitch from spare needle) and turn. Distribute all 28 [30:32] sts over 3 needles and, using 4th needle, now work in rounds again and shape foot as follows: Starting with row 26 of chart, work 24 [26:26] rounds, ending after chart row 48 [50:50].

Shape toe

Break off green and lilac and complete sock using cream *only*.

Work 0 [0:2] rounds.

next round (Sl 1, K1, psso, K10 [11:12], K2tog) twice. 24 [26:28] sts.

next round Knit.

next round (Sl 1, K1, psso, K8 [9:10], K2tog) twice. 20 [22:24] sts.

next round Knit.

next round (Sl 1, K1, psso, K6 [7:8], K2tog) twice. 16 [18:20] sts.

next round Knit.

Slip first 8 [9:10] sts onto one needle and last 8 [9:10] sts onto another needle. Graft the 2 sets of 8 [9:10] sts together to close toe seam.

Left sock

Work as for Right Sock to start of heel shaping.

Shape heel

row 1 (RS) Using cream, K27 [29:31], wrap next st (by slipping next st from left needle onto right needle, taking yarn to opposite side of work between needles and then slipping same st back onto left needle – when working back across wrapped sts, work the wrapped st together with any wrapped loops) and turn.

Slip first 14 [15:16] sts of last complete round onto a spare needle and now working in rows, not rounds, work on rem set of 14 [15:16] sts only for heel using cream *only* as follows:

Work rows 2 to 16 as given for Right Sock. Distribute all 28 [30:32] sts over 3 needles and, using 4th needle, now work in rounds again and shape foot as follows: Starting with row 22 of chart, work 23 [25:25] rounds, ending after chart row 48 [50:50].

Complete as given for Right Sock from start of toe shaping.

Finishing

Press carefully following instructions on yarn label.

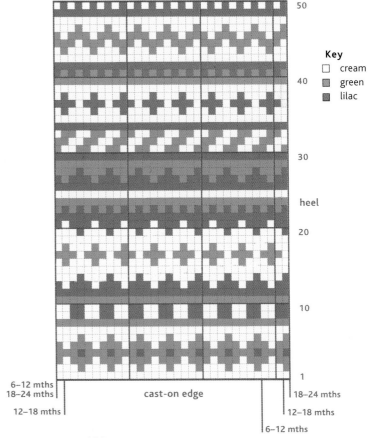

Key
- □ cream
- ▨ green
- ▨ lilac

50

40

30

heel

20

10

1

6–12 mths
18–24 mths

12–18 mths

cast-on edge

18–24 mths

12–18 mths

6–12 mths

socks in a box

The perfect present for any new baby! Seven jolly pairs of cotton socks all neatly packaged in a box – that's one pair for each day of the week.

materials
One 50 g (1¾ oz) ball of Rowan Cotton Glace in each of white (Bleached 726), yellow (Buttercup 825), blue (Maritime 817), green (Shoot 814), red (Poppy 741), purple (Excite 815) and pink (In The Pink 819)

needles
Set of 4 double-pointed 3.25 mm (UK 10) (US size 3) knitting needles

sizes
to fit age 0–3 [3–6:6–12:12–18] mths
length of foot 8.5 [9:9.5:10] cm (3¼ [3½:3¾:4] in)

tension/gauge
23 sts and 32 rows to 10 cm (4 in) measured over stocking (stockinette) st using 3.25 mm (US size 3) needles.

special note
All pairs use one colour for the trim (rib, heel and toe) and another for the main sections. For first pair, use purple for the trim and pink for the main sections. For second pair, use white and purple. For third pair, use green and white. For fourth pair, use red and green. For fifth pair, use blue and red. For sixth pair, use yellow and blue. For seventh pair, use pink and yellow.

abbreviations
K knit; P purl; psso pass slipped stitch over; rem remaining; rep repeat; RS right side; sl 1 slip one stitch; st(s) stitch(es); stocking (stockinette) st RS rows K, WS rows P; tog together; 0 no stitches worked for this size; g grams; oz ounces; mm millimetres; mths months; cm centimetres; in inches.

socks in a box

Right sock

Using trim colour, cast on 22 [24:26:28] sts. Distribute these sts over 3 of the needles and, using 4th needle, work in rounds as follows:

round 1 (RS) *K1, P1, rep from * to end. Rep this round 4 times more.
Break off trim colour and join in main colour.

round 6 Knit.
This round forms stocking (stockinette) st. Work in stocking (stockinette) st for 10 [11:12:13] more rounds.

Shape heel

Slip last 11 [12:13:14] sts of last round onto a spare needle.
**Join in trim colour.
Using trim colour and now working in rows, not rounds, work on rem set of 11 [12:13:14] sts only for heel as follows:
row 1 (RS) K11 [12:13:14].
row 2 Sl 1, P9 [10:11:12], wrap next st (by slipping next st from left needle onto right needle, taking yarn to opposite side of work between needles and then slipping same st back onto left needle – when working back across wrapped sts, work the wrapped st together with any wrapped loops) and turn.
row 3 Sl 1, K8 [9:10:11], wrap next st and turn.
row 4 Sl 1, P7 [8:9:10], wrap next st and turn.
row 5 Sl 1, K6 [7:8:9], wrap next st and turn.
row 6 Sl 1, P5 [6:7:8], wrap next st and turn.
row 7 Sl 1, K4 [5:6:7], wrap next st and turn.

row 8 Rep row 6.
row 9 Rep row 5.
row 10 Rep row 4.
row 11 Rep row 3.
row 12 Rep row 2.
row 13 Sl 1, K10 [11:12:13].
Break off trim colour.
Distribute all 22 [24:26:28] sts over 3 needles and, using 4th needle, now work in rounds again using main colour and shape foot as follows:
Work in stocking (stockinette) st for 14 [15:16:17] rounds.

Shape toe

Break off main colour and join in trim colour.
rounds 1 and 2 Knit.
round 3 (Sl 1, K1, psso, K7 [8:9:10], K2tog) twice. 18 [20:22:24] sts.
round 4 Knit.

round 5 (Sl 1, K1, psso, K5 [6:7:8], K2tog) twice. 14 [16:18:20] sts.
round 6 (Sl 1, K1, psso, K3 [4:5:6], K2tog) twice. 10 [12:14:16] sts.
Slip next 5 [6:7:8] sts onto one needle and rem 5 [6:7:8] sts onto another needle. Graft the 2 sets of 5 [6:7:8] sts together to close toe seam.

Left sock

Work as given for Right Sock to start of heel shaping.

Shape heel

Slip *first* 11 [12:13:14] sts of last complete round onto a spare needle.
Complete as given for Right Sock from **.

Finishing

Press carefully following instructions on yarn label.

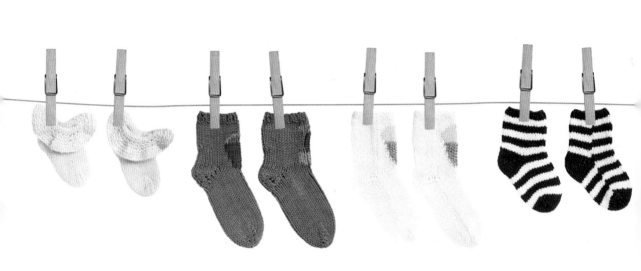

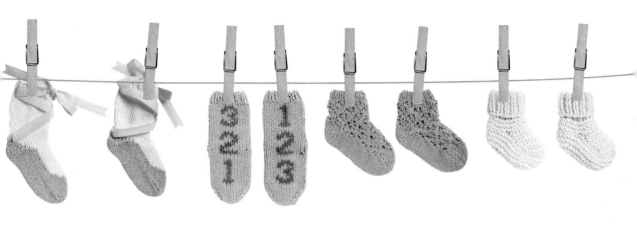

fun for feet

frilly tops

An easy-to-knit frilled top adds a pretty touch to these simple little ankle socks. They are knitted on four needles in a luxurious cashmere blend yarn that is soft enough for the most sensitive of tiny toes.

materials
One 50 g (1¾ oz) ball of Rowan RYC Cashsoft DK
in cream (Cream 500)

needles
Set of 4 double-pointed 4 mm (UK 8) (US size 6)
knitting needles

sizes
to fit age 0–3 [3–6:6–12:12–18] mths
length of foot 8.5 [9:9.5:10] cm (3¼ [3½:3¾:4] in)

tension/gauge
22 sts and 30 rows to 10 cm (4 in) measured over stocking
(stockinette) st using 4 mm (US size 6) needles.

abbreviations
K knit; P purl; **psso** pass slipped stitch over; **rem** remaining;
rep repeat; **RS** right side; **sl 1** slip one stitch;
st(s) stitch(es); **stocking (stockinette) st** RS rows K, WS
rows P; **tog** together; **WS** wrong side; **g** grams; **oz** ounces;
mm millimetres; **mths** months;
cm centimetres; **in** inches.

frilly tops

Socks

(both alike)

Cast on 66 [72:78:84] sts.

Distribute these sts over 3 of the needles and, using 4th needle, work in rounds as follows:

round 1 (RS) Purl.

round 2 Knit.

rounds 3 and 4 Rep rounds 1 and 2.

round 5 Purl.

round 6 *K2tog, K1, rep from * to end. 44 [48:52:56] sts.

rounds 7 and 8 Rep rounds 1 and 2.

round 9 Purl.

round 10 *K2tog, rep from * to end. 22 [24:26:28] sts.

round 11 Purl.

These 11 rounds complete frill.

round 12 Knit.

This round forms stocking (stockinette) st. Work in stocking (stockinette) st for 5 [6:7:8] rounds more.

Shape heel

row 1 (RS) K4 [5:5:6], wrap next st (by slipping next st from left needle onto right needle, taking yarn to opposite side of work between needles and then slipping same st back onto left needle – when working back across wrapped sts, work the wrapped st together with any wrapped loops) and turn. Slip next 11 [12:13.14] sts of last complete round onto a spare needle and now working in rows, not rounds, work on rem set of 11 [12:13:14] sts only for heel as follows:

row 2 Sl 1, P8 [9:10:11], wrap next st and turn.

row 3 Sl 1, K7 [8:9:10], wrap next st and turn.

row 4 Sl 1, P6 [7:8:9], wrap next st and turn.

row 5 Sl 1, K5 [6:7:8], wrap next st and turn.

row 6 Sl 1, P4 [5:6:7], wrap next st and turn.

row 7 Rep row 5.

row 8 Rep row 4.

row 9 Rep row 3.

row 10 Rep row 2.

row 11 Sl 1, K9 [10:11:12], wrap next st and turn.

row 12 Sl 1, P10 [11:12:13], wrap next st (first stitch from spare needle) and turn.

row 13 Sl 1, K5 [5:6:6].

Distribute all 22 [24:26:28] sts over 3 needles and, using 4th needle, now work in rounds again and shape foot as follows:

Work 16 [17:18:19] rounds.

Shape toe

round 1 K3 [4:4:5], K2tog, sl 1, K1, psso, K7 [8:9:10], K2tog, sl 1, K1, psso, K4 [4:5:5]. 18 [20:22:24] sts.

round 2 Knit.

round 3 K2 [3:3:4], K2tog, sl 1, K1, psso, K5 [6:7:8], K2tog, sl 1, K1, psso, K3 [3:4:4]. 14 [16:18:20] sts.

round 4 Knit.

round 5 K1 [2:2:3], K2tog, sl 1, K1, psso, K3 [4:5:6], K2tog, sl 1, K1, psso, K2 [2:3:3]. 10 [12:14:16] sts.

round 6 Knit.

round 7 K2 [3:3:4].

Slip next 5 [6:7:8] sts onto one needle and rem 5 [6:7:8] sts onto another needle. Graft the 2 sets of 5 [6:7:8] sts together to close toe seam.

Finishing

Press carefully following instructions on yarn label.

seaside socks

He won't forget his bucket and spade next time he goes to the seaside in these little socks! They are worked on four needles in a robust cotton yarn, and the motifs are embroidered on later.

materials

One 50 g (1³⁄₄ oz) ball of Rowan Handknit Cotton in blue (Bermuda 324)

Small amount of same yarn in each of orange (Flame 254) and green (Gooseberry 219) for embroidery

needles

Set of 4 double-pointed 4mm (UK 8) (US size 6) knitting needles

sizes

to fit age 18 mths–2 yrs [2–3 yrs:3–4 yrs]

length of foot 12.5 [13.5:14.5] cm (5 [5¹⁄₄:5³⁄₄] in)

tension/gauge

20 sts and 28 rows to 10 cm (4 in) measured over stocking (stockinette) st using 4 mm (US size 6) needles.

abbreviations

K knit; P purl; psso pass slipped stitch over; rem remaining; rep repeat; RS right side; sl 1 slip one stitch; st(s) stitch(es); stocking (stockinette) st RS rows K, WS rows P; tog together; WS wrong side; g grams; oz ounces; mm millimetres; mths months; yrs years; cm centimetres; in inches.

seaside socks

Socks
(both alike)
Using blue, cast on 24 [26:28] sts.
Distribute these sts over 3 of the needles and, using 4th needle, work in rounds as follows:

round 1 (RS) *K1, P1, rep from * to end.
Rep this round twice more.

round 4 Knit.
This round forms stocking (stockinette) st.
Work in stocking (stockinette) st for 10 more rounds.

round 15 K4 [4:5], K2tog, K1 [2:1], sl 1, K1, psso, K15 [16:18]. 22 [24:26] sts.
Work 5 rounds.

Shape heel
row 1 (RS) K11 [12:13] and turn.
Now working in rows, not rounds, work 5 rows on this set of 11 [12:13] sts only, ending after a WS row.

next row (RS) K6 [7:8], sl 1, K1, psso and turn.

next row P2 [3:4], P2tog and turn.

next row K2 [3:4], sl 1, K1, psso and turn.
Rep last 2 rows twice more, then first of these 2 rows again, ending after a WS row.
3 [4:5] sts.
Break off yarn.
Now working in rounds again, start to shape for foot as follows:

next round Pick up and knit 4 sts up first side of heel, K3 [4:5] heel sts, pick up and knit 4 sts down second side of heel, K to end of round. 22 [24:26] sts.
Distribute sts over 3 needles and, using 4th needle, now work in rounds again and shape foot as follows:

Work in stocking (stockinette) st for 23 [25:27] rounds.

Shape toe
round 1 (Sl 1, K1, psso, K7 [8:9], K2tog) twice. 18 [20:22] sts.

round 2 Knit.

round 3 (Sl 1, K1, psso, K5 [6:7], K2tog) twice. 14 [16:18] sts.

round 4 Knit.

round 5 (Sl 1, K1, psso, K3 [4:5], K2tog) twice. 10 [12:14] sts.

round 6 Knit.
Slip first 5 [6:7] sts onto one needle and last 5 [6:7] sts onto another needle. Graft the 2 sets of 5 [6:7] sts together to close toe seam.

Finishing
Following chart, Swiss darn (duplicate stitch) motifs onto socks – place charts centrally on top of foot starting 5 rounds down from cast-on edge.
Press carefully following instructions on yarn label.

cast-on edge   cast-on edge

16   16

10   10

1   1

Key
☐ blue
■ red (Swiss darning)
▨ green (Swiss darning)

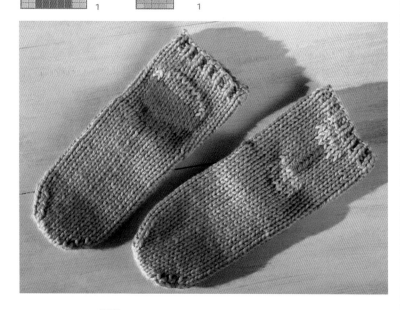

strawberry ice cream

Next time your little one screams for ice cream, give her these
cute socks! They are worked in a pure wool yarn on two needles,
and the cone motif is knitted in as the sock is made.

materials

One 50 g (1¾ oz) ball of Rowan 4-Ply Soft
in cream (Nippy 376)
Small amount of same yarn in each of pink (Fairy 395)
and beige (Linseed 393)

needles

Pair of 3.25 mm (UK 10) (US size 3) knitting needles

sizes

to fit age 18 mths–2 yrs [2–3 yrs:3–4 yrs]
length of foot 12.5 [13.5:14.5] cm (5 [5¼:5¾] in)

tension/gauge

28 sts and 36 rows to 10 cm (4 in) measured over stocking
(stockinette) st using 3.25 mm (US size 3) needles.

abbreviations

K knit; P purl; psso pass slipped stitch over; rem remaining;
rep repeat; RS right side; sl 1 slip one stitch;
st(s) stitch(es); stocking (stockinette) st RS rows K, WS
rows P; tog together; WS wrong side; g grams; oz ounces;
mm millimetres; mths months; yrs years;
cm centimetres; in inches.

strawberry ice cream

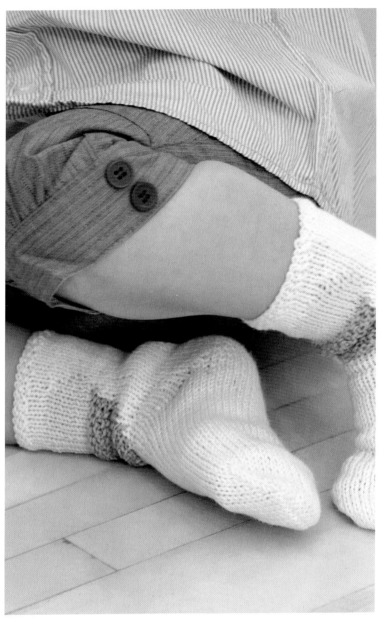

Left sock

Using cream, cast on 42 [44:46] sts.

row 1 (RS) *K1, P1, rep from * to end.

row 2 *P1, K1, rep from * to end.

Rep last 2 rows once more.

Starting with a K row, work in stocking (stockinette) st for 4 rows, ending after a WS row.**

Using a separate ball of yarn for each block of colour and twisting yarns together on WS where they meet to avoid holes forming, now place motif chart as follows:

row 9 (RS) K3 [3:4], work next 15 sts as row 1 of chart, reading chart from right to left, K to end.

row 10 P24 [26:27], work next 15 sts as row 2 of chart, reading chart from left to right, P to end.

These 2 rows set position of chart.

Keeping chart correct, cont as follows:

Work 12 rows.

row 23 (RS) Patt 27 [28:30] sts, K2tog, K2 [3:2], sl 1, K1, psso, K to end. 40 [42:44] sts.

Work 9 rows.

row 33 (RS) Patt 26 [27:29] sts, K2tog, K2 [3:2], sl 1, K1, psso, K to end. 38 [40:42] sts.

Work 3 rows. (All 28 rows of chart now completed.)

Working in stocking (stockinette) st using cream only, complete sock as follows:

Work 4 rows, ending after a WS row.

Shape heel

row 1 (RS) K to last 2 sts, wrap next st (by slipping next st from left needle onto right needle, taking yarn to opposite side of work between needles and then slipping same st back onto left needle – when working back across wrapped sts, work the wrapped st together with any wrapped loops) and turn.

***row 2** Sl 1, P15 [16:17], wrap next st and turn.

row 3 Sl 1, K14 [15:16], wrap next st and turn.

row 4 Sl 1, P13 [14:15], wrap next st and turn.

row 5 Sl 1, K12 [13:14], wrap next st and turn.

row 6 Sl 1, P11 [12:13], wrap next st and turn.

row 7 Sl 1, K10 [11:12], wrap next st and turn.

row 8 Sl 1, P9 [10:11], wrap next st and turn.

row 9 Rep row 7.

row 10 Rep row 6.

row 11 Rep row 5.

row 12 Rep row 4.

row 13 Rep row 3.

row 14 Rep row 2.

row 15 Sl 1, K16 [17:18], wrap next st and turn.

row 16 Sl 1, P17 [18:19], wrap next st and turn.

row 17 Sl 1, K to end.

Starting with a P row, work 31 [35:39] rows, ending after a WS row.

Shape toe

row 1 (RS) K1, (sl 1, K1, psso, K14 [15:16], K2tog) twice, K1. 34 [36:38] sts.

row 2 Purl.

row 3 K1, (sl 1, K1, psso, K12 [13:14], K2tog) twice, K1. 30 [32:34] sts.

row 4 Purl.

row 5 K1, (sl 1, K1, psso, K10 [11:12], K2tog) twice, K1. 26 [28:30] sts.

row 6 Purl.

row 7 K1, (sl 1, K1, psso, K8 [9:10], K2tog) twice, K1. 22 [24:26] sts.

row 8 Purl.

Cast (bind) off.

Right sock

Work as given for Left Sock to **.

Using a separate ball of yarn for each block of colour and twisting yarns together on WS where they meet to avoid holes forming, now place motif chart as follows:

row 9 (RS) K24 [26:27], work next 15 sts as row 1 of chart, reading chart from left to right (to reverse motif), K to end.

row 10 P3 [3:4], work next 15 sts as row 2 of chart, reading chart right to left, P to end.

These 2 rows set position of chart.

Keeping chart correct, cont as follows:

Work 12 rows.

row 23 (RS) K9 [9:10], K2tog, K2 [3:2], sl 1, K1, psso, patt to end. 40 [42:44] sts.

Work 9 rows.

row 33 (RS) K8 [8:9], K2tog, K2 [3:2], sl 1, K1, psso, patt to end. 38 [40:42] sts.

Work 3 rows. (All 28 rows of chart now completed.)

Working in stocking (stockinette) st using cream only, complete sock as follows:

Work 4 rows, ending after a WS row.

Shape heel

row 1 (RS) K18 [19:20], wrap next st and turn.

Complete as given for Left Sock from ***.

Finishing

Press carefully following instructions on yarn label.

Sew inside leg, foot and toe seams.

cast-on edge

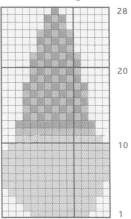

Key

☐ cream (K on RS rows, P on WS rows)

▨ pink (K on RS rows, P on WS rows)

▨ beige (K on RS rows, P on WS rows)

▨ beige (P on RS rows, K on WS rows)

sailor stripes

Go nautical with these jolly sailor striped socks! Knitted in a soft, easy-care cotton blend yarn using four needles, they are really quick to make. Use the classic navy and cream or, if you prefer, pretty pastels.

materials

One 50 g (1¾ oz) ball of Rowan Calmer in each of navy (Slosh 479) and cream (Drift 460)

needles

Set of 4 double-pointed 3.75 mm (UK 9) (US size 5) knitting needles

sizes

to fit age 6–12 [12–18:18–24] mths
length of foot 9.5 [10:10.5] cm (3¾ [4:4¼] in)

tension/gauge

23 sts and 34 rows to 10 cm (4 in) measured over stocking (stockinette) st using 3.75 mm (US size 5) needles.

abbreviations

K knit; P purl; psso pass slipped stitch over; rem remaining; rep repeat; RS right side; sl 1 slip one stitch; st(s) stitch(es); stocking (stockinette) st RS rows K, WS rows P; tog together; g grams; oz ounces; mm millimetres; mths months; cm centimetres; in inches.

sailor stripes

Right sock

Using navy, cast on 30 [32:34] sts.
Distribute these sts over 3 of the needles
and, using 4th needle, work in rounds
as follows:

round 1 (RS) *K1, P1, rep from * to end.
Rep this round 3 times more.
Join in cream.

rounds 5 to 8 Using cream, work in
stocking (stockinette) st.

rounds 9 to 12 Using navy, work in stocking (stockinette) st.

Last 8 rounds form striped stocking (stockinette) st.

Keeping stripes correct, work as follows:
Work 14 rounds, ending after 2 rounds
using navy.

Shape heel

row 1 (RS) Using navy, K14 [15:16], wrap
next st (by slipping next st from left needle
onto right needle, taking yarn to opposite
side of work between needles and then
slipping same st back onto left needle –
when working back across wrapped sts,
work the wrapped st together with any
wrapped loops) and turn.

Slip next 15 [16:17] sts of last complete
round onto a spare needle and now working in rows, not rounds, work on rem set of
15 [16:17] sts only for heel using navy *only*
as follows:

row 2 Sl 1, P12 [13:14], wrap next st
and turn.

row 3 Sl 1, K11 [12:13], wrap next st
and turn.

row 4 Sl 1, P10 [11:12], wrap next st
and turn.

row 5 Sl 1, K9 [10:11], wrap next st and
turn.

row 6 Sl 1, P8 [9:10], wrap next st and turn.

row 7 Sl 1, K7 [8:9], wrap next st and turn.

row 8 Sl 1, P6 [7:8], wrap next st and turn.

row 9 Rep row 7.

row 10 Rep row 6.

row 11 Rep row 5.

row 12 Rep row 4.

row 13 Rep row 3.

row 14 Rep row 2.

row 15 Sl 1, K13 [14:15], wrap next st
and turn.

row 16 Sl 1, P14 [15:16], wrap next st (first
stitch from spare needle) and turn.

Distribute all 30 [32:34] sts over 3 needles
and, using 4th needle, now work in rounds
again and shape foot as follows:

Starting with 2 more rows using navy and
then 4 rows using cream, work in striped
stocking (stockinette) st for 22 [22:26]
rounds, ending after 4 rows using cream
[cream:navy].

Shape toe

Break off cream [cream:navy] and complete
sock using navy [navy:cream] *only*.
Work 0 [2:0] rounds.

next round (Sl 1, K1, psso, K11 [12:13],
K2tog) twice. 26 [28:30] sts.

next round Knit.

next round (Sl 1, K1, psso, K9 [10:11],
K2tog) twice. 22 [24:26] sts.

next round Knit.

next round (Sl 1, K1, psso, K7 [8:9], K2tog)
twice. 18 [20:22] sts.

next round Knit.

Slip first 9 [10:11] sts onto one needle and
last 9 [10:11] sts onto another needle. Graft

the 2 sets of 9 [10:11] sts together to close
toe seam.

Left sock

Work as given for Right Sock to start of
heel shaping.

Shape heel

row 1 (RS) Using navy, K29 [31:33],
wrap next st (by slipping next st from left
needle onto right needle, taking yarn to
opposite side of work between needles
and then slipping same st back onto
left needle – when working back across
wrapped sts, work the wrapped st
together with any wrapped loops) and
turn.

Slip first 15 [16:17] sts of last complete
round onto a spare needle and now working
in rows, not rounds, work on rem set of
15 [16:17] sts only for heel using navy *only*
as follows:

Work rows 2 to 16 as given for Right Sock.
Distribute all 30 [32:34] sts over 3 needles
and, using 4th needle, now work in rounds
again and shape foot as follows:

Starting with 1 more row using navy and
then 4 rows using cream, work in striped
stocking (stockinette) st for 21 [21:25]
rounds, ending after 4 rows using cream
[cream:navy].

Complete as given for Right Sock from
start of toe shaping.

Finishing

Press carefully following instructions on
yarn label.

ballet shoes

Transform your little angel into a ballerina with these sweet ballet shoe-style socks. They are worked on two needles in a luxurious yarn, and shiny taffeta ribbons are laced through knitted eyelet holes.

materials
One 50 g (1¾ oz) ball of Rowan RYC Luxury Cotton DK
in each of white (Bleached 258)
and pink (Damsel 251)

extras
180 cm (71 in) of 13 mm (½ in) wide taffeta ribbon

needles
Pair of 4 mm (UK 8) (US size 6) knitting needles

sizes
to fit age 6–12 [12–18:18–24] mths
length of foot 9.5 [10:10.5] cm (3¾ [4:4 ¼] in)

tension/gauge
22 sts and 30 rows to 10 cm (4 in) measured over stocking
(stockinette) st using 4 mm (US size 6) needles.

abbreviations
K knit; P purl; psso pass slipped stitch over; rem remaining;
rep repeat; RS right side; sl 1 slip one stitch; st(s) stitch(es);
stocking (stockinette) st RS rows K, WS rows P;
tbl through back of loops; tog together; WS wrong side;
yfwd yarn forward – bring yarn forward between needles
and over right needle to make a new stitch (US yarn over);
0 no stitches worked for this size; g grams; oz ounces;
mm millimetres; mths months; cm centimetres; in inches.

ballet shoes

Right sock

Using white, cast on 32 [34:36] sts.

row 1 (RS) *K1, P1, rep from * to end.
Rep this row 3 times more.

row 5 K8 [8:9], yfwd, (sl 1, K2tog, psso)
1 [0:1] times, (K2tog, sl 1, K1, psso) 0 [1:0]
times, yfwd, K21 [22:24].

Starting with a P row, work in stocking
(stockinette) st for 11 rows, ending after a
WS row.

row 17 K7 [8:8], K2tog, K1 [0:1], sl 1, K1,
psso, K20 [22:23]. 30 [32:34] sts.
Work 7 rows.

row 25 K6 [7:7], K2tog, K1 [0:1], sl 1, K1,
psso, K19 [21:22]. 28 [30:32] sts.
Work 5 rows, ending after a WS row.

Shape heel

Break off white and join in pink.
Using pink only for heel, work as follows:

row 1 (RS) K6 [6:7], yfwd, (sl 1, K2tog,
psso) 1 [0:1] times, (K2tog, sl 1, K1, psso) 0
[1:0] times, yfwd, K4 [4:5], wrap next st (by
slipping next st from left needle onto right
needle, taking yarn to opposite side of work
between needles and then slipping same st
back onto left needle – when working back
across wrapped sts, work the wrapped st
together with any wrapped loops) and turn.

row 2 Sl 1, P10 [11:12], wrap next st and
turn.

row 3 Sl 1, K9 [10:11], wrap next st and
turn.

row 4 Sl 1, P8 [9:10], wrap next st and
turn.

row 5 Sl 1, K7 [8:9], wrap next st and turn.

row 6 Sl 1, P6 [7:8], wrap next st and turn.

row 7 Sl 1, K5 [6:7], wrap next st and turn.

row 8 Sl 1, P4 [5:6], wrap next st and turn.

row 9 Rep row 7.

row 10 Rep row 6.

row 11 Rep row 5.

row 12 Rep row 4.

row 13 Rep row 3.

row 14 Rep row 2.

row 15 Sl 1, K11 [12:13], wrap next st
(first stitch from spare needle) and turn.

row 16 Sl 1, P12 [13:14], wrap next st
and turn.

ballet shoes

Shape foot

Using a separate ball of yarn for each block of colour and twisting yarns together on WS where they meet to avoid holes forming, now work as follows:

row 1 Using pink, sl 1, K14 [15:16], using white K11 [12:13], using pink K2.

row 2 Using pink P3, using white P9 [10:11], using pink P16 [17:18].

row 3 Using pink K16 [17:18], using white K9 [10:11], using pink K3.

Rep last 2 rows 5 [6:7] times more.

next row Using pink P4, using white P7 [8:9], using pink P17 [18:19].

next row Using pink K18 [19:20], using white K5 [6:7], using pink K5.

next row Using pink P6, using white P3 [4:5], using pink P19 [20:21].

Break off white and complete sock using pink *only*.

Work 4 rows, ending after a WS row.

Shape toe

row 1 (RS) K1, (sl 1, K1, psso, K9 [10:11], K2tog) twice, K1. 24 [26:28] sts.

row 2 Purl.

row 3 K1, (sl 1, K1, psso, K7 [8:9], K2tog) twice, K1. 20 [22:24] sts.

row 4 Purl.

row 5 K1, (sl 1, K1, psso, K5 [6:7], K2tog) twice, K1. 16 [18:20] sts.

row 6 P1, (P2tog, P3 [4:5], P2tog tbl) twice, P1. 12 [14:16] sts.

Cast (bind) off.

Left sock

Using white, cast on 32 [34:36] sts.

row 1 (RS) *P1, K1, rep from * to end. Rep this row 3 times more.

row 5 K21 [22:24], yfwd, (sl 1, K2tog, psso) 1 [0:1] times, (K2tog, sl 1, K1, psso) 0 [1:0] times, yfwd, K8 [8:9].

Starting with a P row, work in stocking (stockinette) st for 11 rows, ending after a WS row.

row 17 K20 [22:23], K2tog, K1 [0:1], sl 1, K1, psso, K7 [8:8]. 30 [32:34] sts.

Work 7 rows.

row 25 K19 [21:22], K2tog, K1 [0:1], sl 1, K1, psso, K6 [7:7]. 28 [30:32] sts.

Work 5 rows, ending after a WS row.

Shape heel

Using a separate ball of yarn for each block of colour and twisting yarns together on WS where they meet to avoid holes forming, now work as follows:

row 1 (RS) Using pink K2, using white K11 [12:13], using pink K6 [6:7], yfwd, (sl 1, K2tog, psso) 1 [0:1] times, (K2tog, sl 1, K1, psso) 0 [1:0] times, yfwd, K4 [4:5], wrap next st (by slipping next st from left needle onto right needle, taking yarn to opposite side of work between needles and then slipping same st back onto left needle – when working back across wrapped sts, work the wrapped st together with any wrapped loops) and turn.

Using pink *only* for heel, work heel rows 2 to 16 as given for Right Sock.

Shape foot

row 1 Using pink, sl 1, K to end.

row 2 Using pink P16 [17:18], using white P9 [10:11], using pink P3.

row 3 Using pink K3, using white K9 [10:11], using pink K16 [17:18].

Rep last 2 rows 5 [6:7] times more.

next row Using pink P17 [18:19], using

white P7 [8:9], using pink P4.

next row Using pink K5, using white K5 [6:7], using pink K18 [19:20].

next row Using pink P19 [20:21], using white P3 [4:5], using pink P6.

Break off white and complete sock using pink *only*.

Work 4 rows, ending after a WS row.

Complete sock as given for Right Sock from start of toe shaping.

Finishing

Press carefully following instructions on yarn label.

Sew inside leg, foot and toe seams. Cut ribbon into two equal lengths and thread through eyelet holes in first row in pink at back of heel. Wrap ribbon around leg section as in photograph and thread ends through eyelet holes in first row after rib at top of sock. Tie ribbon ends in a bow at centre front.

as easy as 1, 2, 3

Have fun making up your own colour combinations for these tiny cotton socks. They are knitted on four needles in just one colour, and the numbers are embroidered on when they are finished. What could be easier?

materials
One 50 g (1¾ oz) ball of Rowan Cotton Glace in aqua (Pier 809)
Small amount of same yarn in lilac (Hyacinth 787) for embroidery

needles
Set of 4 double-pointed 3.25 mm (UK 10) (US size 3) knitting needles

sizes
to fit age 0–3 [3–6:6–12:12–18] mths
length of foot 8.5 [9:9.5:10] cm (3¼ [3½:3¾:4] in)

tension/gauge
23 sts and 32 rows to 10 cm (4 in) measured over stocking (stockinette) st using 3.25 mm (US size 3) needles.

abbreviations
K knit; P purl; psso pass slipped stitch over; rem remaining; rep repeat; RS right side; sl 1 slip one stitch; st(s) stitch(es); stocking (stockinette) st RS rows K, WS rows P; tog together; g grams; oz ounces; mm millimetres; mths months; cm centimetres; in inches.

as easy as 1, 2, 3

Right sock

Using aqua, cast on 24 [26:28:30] sts. Distribute these sts over 3 of the needles and, using 4th needle, work in rounds as follows:

round 1 (RS) *K1, P1, rep from * to end. Rep this round 3 times more.

round 5 Knit.

Rep last round 18 [19:20:21] times more.

Shape heel

row 1 (RS) Sl 1, K10 [11:12:13], wrap next st (by slipping next st from left needle onto right needle, taking yarn to opposite side of work between needles and then slipping same st back onto left needle – when working back across wrapped sts, work the wrapped st together with any wrapped loops) and turn.

Slip last 12 [13:14:15] sts of last complete round onto a spare needle and now working in rows, not rounds, work on first set of 12 [13:14:15] sts only for heel as follows:

row 2 Sl 1, P9 [10:11:12], wrap next st and turn.

row 3 Sl 1, K8 [9:10:11], wrap next st and turn.

row 4 Sl 1, P7 [8:9:10], wrap next st and turn.

row 5 Sl 1, K6 [7:8:9], wrap next st and turn.

row 6 Sl 1, P5 [6:7:8], wrap next st and turn.

row 7 Rep row 5.

row 8 Rep row 4.

row 9 Rep row 3.

row 10 Rep row 2.

row 11 Rep row 1.

row 12 Sl 1, P11 [12:13:14], wrap next st

(first stitch from spare needle) and turn. Distribute all 24 [26:28:30] sts over 3 needles and, using 4th needle, now work in rounds again and shape foot as follows:

next round (RS) Knit.

Rep last round 15 [17:19:21] times more.

Shape toe

round 1 (Sl 1, K1, psso, K8 [9:10:11], K2tog) twice. 20 [22:24:26] sts.

round 2 Knit.

round 3 (Sl 1, K1, psso, K6 [7:8:9], K2tog) twice. 16 [18:20:22] sts.

round 4 Knit.

round 5 (Sl 1, K1, psso, K4 [5:6:7], K2tog) twice. 12 [14:16:18] sts.

round 6 Knit.

Slip first 6 [7:8:9] sts onto one needle and rem 6 [7:8:9] sts onto another needle. Graft the 2 sets of 6 [7:8:9] sts together to close toe seam.

Left sock

Work as given for Right Sock to start of heel shaping.

Shape heel

row 1 (RS) K12 [13:14:15], sl 1, K10 [11:12:13], wrap next st and turn.

Slip first 12 [13:14:15] sts of last complete round onto a spare needle and now working in rows, not rounds, work on last set of 12 [13:14:15] sts only for heel as follows:

Work rows 2 to 12 of heel shaping as given for Right Sock.

row 13 K12 [13:14:15].

Distribute all 24 [26:28:30] sts over 3 needles and, using 4th needle, now work in rounds again and shape foot as follows:

next round (RS) Knit.

Rep last round 14 [16:18:20] times more. Complete as given for Right Sock from start of toe shaping.

Finishing

Following charts, Swiss darn (duplicate stitch) numbers onto front of socks using lilac – place top of chart 5 [6:7:8] rows down from cast-on edge and position chart centrally.

Press carefully following instructions on yarn label.

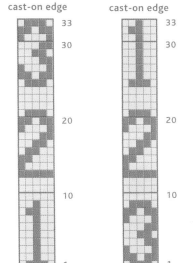

cast-on edge   cast-on edge

33   33
30   30
20   20
10   10
1   1

Key

☐ aqua
▨ lilac

lacy socks

Delight any little girl with this pretty pair of lacy ankle socks.
Knitted on four needles using a luxury silk and wool mix yarn, the lacy
pattern is surprisingly quick and easy to knit.

materials

One 50 g (1³/₄ oz) ball of Rowan RYC Silk Wool DK
in lilac (Geranium 310)

needles

Set of 4 double-pointed 3.25 mm (UK 10) (US size 3)
knitting needles

sizes

to fit age 18 mths–2 yrs [3–4 yrs]
length of foot 12.5 [14.5] cm (5 [5³/₄ in)

tension/gauge

23 sts and 32 rows to 10 cm (4 in) measured over stocking
(stockinette) st using 3.25 mm (US size 3) needles.

abbreviations

cont continue; K knit; P purl; patt pattern;
psso pass slipped stitch over; rem remaining; rep repeat; RS
right side; sl 1 slip one stitch; st(s) stitch(es);
tog together; yfwd yarn forward – bring yarn forward
between needles and over right needle to make a new
stitch (US yarn over); g grams; oz ounces; mm millimetres;
mths months; yrs years; cm centimetres; in inches.

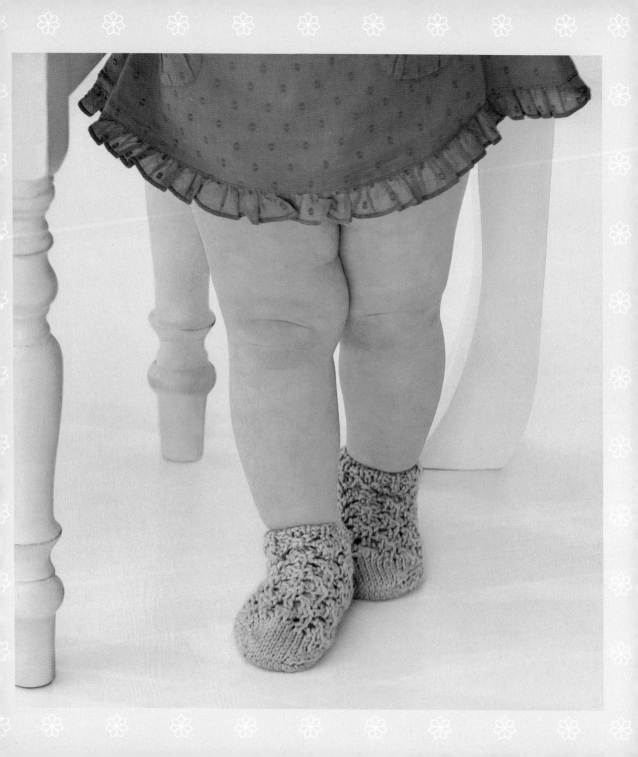

lacy socks

Socks

(both alike)

Cast on 30 [36] sts.

Distribute these sts over 3 of the needles and, using 4th needle, work in rounds as follows:

round 1 (RS) *K1, P1, rep from * to end.
Rep this round twice more.

Now work in lace patt as follows:

round 4 Knit.

round 5 *K1, yfwd, sl 1, K1, psso, K1, K2tog, yfwd, rep from * to end.

round 6 Knit.

round 7 *K1, yfwd, K1, sl 1, K2tog, psso, K1, yfwd, rep from * to end.

round 8 Knit.

round 9 *K1, K2tog, yfwd, K1, yfwd, sl 1, K1, psso, rep from * to end.

round 10 Knit to last st.

round 11 *Sl 1, K2tog, psso, (K1, yfwd) twice, K1, rep from * to end.

Rounds 4 to 11 form patt.

Work in patt for 8 [12] rounds more, ending after patt round 11 [7].

Shape heel

row 1 (RS) K7 [8], wrap next st (by slipping next st from left needle onto right needle, taking yarn to opposite side of work between needles and then slipping same st back onto left needle – when working back across wrapped sts, work the wrapped st together with any wrapped loops) and turn.

Slip next 16 [20] sts of last complete round onto a spare needle and now working in rows, not rounds, work on rem set of 14 [16] sts only for heel as follows:

row 2 Sl 1, P12 [14], wrap next st and turn.

row 3 Sl 1, K11 [13], wrap next st and turn.

row 4 Sl 1, P10 [12], wrap next st and turn.

row 5 Sl 1, K9 [11], wrap next st and turn.

row 6 Sl 1, P8 [10], wrap next st and turn.

row 7 Sl 1, K7 [9], wrap next st and turn.

row 8 Sl 1, P6 [8], wrap next st and turn.

row 9 Rep row 7.

row 10 Rep row 6.

row 11 Rep row 5.

row 12 Rep row 4.

row 13 Rep row 3.

row 14 Rep row 2.

row 15 Sl 1, K13 [15], wrap next st (first stitch from spare needle) and turn.

row 16 Sl 1, P14 [16], wrap next st (from spare needle) and turn.

row 17 Sl 1, K6 [7].

Distribute all 30 [36] sts over 3 needles and, using 4th needle, now work in rounds again and shape foot as follows:

next round (RS) Knit.

next round K7 [10], (yfwd, sl 1, K1, psso, K1, K2tog, yfwd, K1) 3 times, K5 [8].

next round Knit.

next round K7 [10], (yfwd, K1, sl 1, K2tog, psso, K1, yfwd, K1) 3 times, K5 [8].

next round Knit.

next round K7 [10], (K2tog, yfwd, K1, yfwd, sl 1, K1, psso, K1) 3 times, K5 [8].

next round Knit.

next round K6 [9], K2tog, K1, (yfwd, K1, yfwd, K I, sl 1, K2tog, psso, K1) twice, (yfwd, K1) twice, sl 1, K1, psso, K5 [8].

Last 8 rounds form patt for foot section.
Work in patt as now set for 12 [16] rounds more.

next round K30 [9], (sl 1, K1, psso, K15, K2tog, K8) 0 [1] times. 30 [34] sts.

Shape toe

round 1 Knit.

round 2 K6 [7], K2tog, sl 1, K1, psso, K11 [13], K2tog, sl 1, K1, psso, K5 [6]. 26 [30] sts.

round 3 Knit.

round 4 K5 [6], K2tog, sl 1, K1, psso, K9 [11], K2tog, sl 1, K1, psso, K4 [5]. 22 [26] sts.

round 5 Knit.

round 6 K4 [5], K2tog, sl 1, K1, psso, K7 [9], K2tog, sl 1, K1, psso, K3 [4]. 18 [22] sts.

round 7 Knit.

round 8 K5 [6].

Slip next 9 [11] sts onto one needle and rem 9 [11] sts onto another needle. Graft the 2 sets of 9 [11] sts together to close toe seam.

Finishing

Press carefully following instructions on yarn label.

beautiful bootees

These classic bootees have a clever turn-back rib at the top
that fits snugly around baby's ankle to make sure they stay on tiny feet.
Knit them in simple stripes or just one colour to make them even easier.

materials

One 50 g (1¾oz) ball of Rowan RYC Cashsoft Baby DK
in each of lemon (Limone 802)
and white (Snowman 800)

needles

Pair of 3.75 mm (UK 9) (US size 5) knitting needles

sizes

to fit age 0–3 [3–6:6–12:12–18] mths
length of foot 8.5 [9:9.5:10] cm (3¼ [3½:3¾:4] in)

tension/gauge

22 sts and 40 rows to 10 cm (4 in) measured over garter st
using 3.75 mm (US size 5) needles.

abbreviations

dec decrease; K knit; P purl; rem remaining; rep repeat;
RS right side; st(s) stitch(es); tbl through back of loops;
tog together; WS wrong side; g grams; oz ounces;
mm millimetres; mths months;
cm centimetres; in inches.

beautiful bootees

Bootees

(both alike)

Using lemon, cast on 25 [27:29:31] sts.

row 1 (WS) P1, *K1, P1, rep from * to end.

row 2 K1, *P1, K1, rep from * to end.

These 2 rows form rib.

Work in rib for 15 [17:17:19] rows more, dec 1 st at end of last row. 24 [26:28:30] sts.

Join in white.

Now work in striped garter st (K every row) as follows:

Using white, knit 2 rows.

Using lemon, knit 2 rows.

These 4 rows form striped garter st.

Work in striped garter st for 2 rows more, ending after 2 rows using white.

Shape instep

Keeping stripes correct, shape instep as follows:

row 1 (RS) K16 [17:19:20] and turn.

row 2 K8 [8:10:10] and turn.

Work 14 [14:18:18] rows on these 8 [8:10:10] sts only for instep.

Break off yarns.

Rejoin lemon at base of instep, pick up and knit 8 [9:10:11] sts up first side of instep, K across 8 [8:10:10] instep sts, pick up and knit 8 [9:10:11] sts down second side of instep, then K rem 8 [9:9:10] sts. 40 [44:48:52] sts.

Work 7 [9:9:11] rows, ending after a WS row.

Shape sole

Still keeping stripes correct, shape sole as follows:

row 1 (RS) (K2, K2tog, K2tog tbl, K8 [10:12:14], K2tog, K2tog tbl, K2) twice. 32 [36:40:44] sts.

row 2 Knit.

row 3 (K1, K2tog, K2tog tbl, K6 [8:10:12], K2tog, K2tog tbl, K1) twice. 24 [28:32:36] sts.

row 4 Knit.

row 5 (K2tog, K2tog tbl, K4 [6:8:10], K2tog, K2tog tbl) twice. 16 [20:24:28] sts.

row 6 Knit.

Cast (bind) off.

Finishing

Do *not* press.

Sew back and sole seam, reversing seam for turn-back. Fold rib in half to RS around upper edge.

index

acknowledgements

Picture acknowledgements

Photography © Octopus Publishing Group Limited/Adrian Pope

Publisher acknowledgements

The publishers would like to thank the following babies for modelling the socks (and their parents for bringing them along): Adam Nash, Amelia Williamson, Bo Williams-Leedham, Flora Watson, Francis Charlton, Freddie Hunt, Lorelie Moss, Lukas O'Donnell, Maple Pearce, Miles Denny, Natasha Handley, Sorrel Newman and Ziggy Aplin. Thanks also to Angela Bailey for all her assistance with the photoshoot.

Executive editors Katy Denny and Jo Lethaby
Senior editor Fiona Robertson
Pattern checker Susan Horan
Executive art editor Mark Stevens
Designer Beverly Price, One2Six Creative
Stylist Rozelle Bentheim
Senior production controller Manjit Sihra